THE FIRST COMMISSIONER

The Police of New York City

robert l. bryan

Published by robert l. bryan, 2023.

THE FIRST COMMISSIONER

First edition. July 27, 2023.

Copyright © 2023 robert l. bryan.

ISBN: 979-8223113362

Written by robert l. bryan.

For Meghan, the angel on my shoulder.

Prologue:

The New York City Police Department is the largest and one of the oldest municipal police departments in the United States, with approximately 36,000 officers and 19,000 civilian employees.

The NYPD was established in 1845, and today, is responsible for policing an 8.5-million-person city, by performing a wide variety of public safety, law enforcement, traffic management, counterterror, and emergency response roles.

The NYPD is divided into major bureaus for enforcement, investigations, and administration. It has 77 patrol precincts with patrol officers and detectives covering the entire city. The department also has twelve transit districts to police the subway system and its nearly six-million daily riders, and nine police service areas (PSAs) to patrol the city's public housing developments, which are home to more than 400,000 residents. Additionally, uniformed civilians serve as traffic safety agents on the city's busy streets and highways, and as school safety agents, protecting public schools and the over-a-million students who attend them.

Leading this huge force is the police commissioner. Throughout the years there have been many "firsts" in the NYPD, including "firsts" in the position of police commissioner. Keechant Sewell, the current commissioner at the time I am writing this book, was the first female police commissioner. In 1973, Donald Cawley, at 43 years of age, was the youngest person to head the department. In 1983, William Devine had the shortest tenure as police commissioner. He served under Mayor Koch for only two days during the transition from Robert McGuire to Benjamin Ward. In 1984, Benjamin Ward became the first Black police commissioner, and when Richard Enright took the helm of the department in 1918, he became the first commissioner appointed from within the uniformed ranks of the department.

What about the "first" police commissioner? Even though the NYPD as we know it today was established in 1845, the first single-headed police commissioner was not appointed until 1901. Before that a board of between four and six police commissioners controlled the department.

The first police commissioner to run the department alone in 1901 was a rather obscure figure in history who took over a department in turmoil for a relatively short period of time. Yet, his story is unique and interesting, and in some ways, a bit strange. I hope you enjoy.

Introduction:

The New York City Police Department was founded in 1845. Around that same time a force much more powerful than the police was thriving in New York City and would continue to flourish with varying degrees of power until well into the 20th century. This powerhouse behind the New York City government for over a hundred years was called the Society of Saint Tammany, or the Columbian Order. These names, however, were too cumbersome for most New Yorkers who came to know the organization by its meeting place – Tammany Hall.

The club was named after Tamanend, a prominent Native American Chief who had enabled the founding of Pennsylvania by William Penn. With the wave of immigration in the 1840s, mainly from Ireland, the New York establishment argued that America should be for Americans already here and these new arrivals were denied the most basic of opportunities. They needed a voice, and that voice was Tammany Hall – in exchange for votes.

During the 19th century New York City was divided into wards, with an alderman in charge of each ward. The aldermen were responsible for appointing almost all public employees within the ward including police. This meant that when Tammany controlled the city, they could provide jobs for the poor immigrants who voted for them. Tammany politicians made a lot of money from this arrangement. Lower paying jobs were given in return for helping with an election campaign while higher paying jobs were often sold to the highest bidder.

During the waning years of the 19th century the beat from the drums of change and reform were picking up in intensity. William "Boss" Tweed, the infamous leader of Tammany Hall died in 1878 after having been disgraced and imprisoned.[1]

In 1888 a group of wealthy New Yorkers vacationing in Western Massachusetts chanced upon a fiery sermon by a minister extolling the virtues of living a simple, honest life under the administration of a clean government. The New Yorkers were so impressed that they invited the minister to preach in New York City. Thus, began the crusade of Charles Parkhurst, who became the leader of the Society for the Prevention of Crime and an outspoken critic of Tammany Hall and the collusion between the police and organized crime where the cops had become the managers of a vice economy. Parkhurst was the first to use the term "organized crime," which unlike its most common meaning referring to the Mafia, Parkhurst defined organized crime as simply being the government acting in a criminal fashion.

Parkhurst soon learned how powerful Tammany Hall was. Despite his numerous sermons pointing to the corruption of the police and city government, the powers in the city laughed at his rhetoric and ignored him. He was going to have to come up with solid evidence to back up his sermons.

Parkhurst hired private detectives and set out to see the worst New York City had to offer. At the end of two weeks, he gave another sermon, but this time he wasn't just making allegations of corruption. In this sermon he meticulously laid out all the evidence he had uncovered. Still, during the 1890s, Tammany still ruled New York politics under the leadership of Richard Croker.

Richard Croker was born in County Cork, Ireland, in 1843, and immigrated with his family to the United States three years later. They soon settled in New York City, where young Croker sporadically attended the common schools until becoming a machinist's apprentice at the age of 13. A scrappy street fighter, Croker led the Fourth Avenue Tunnel Gang, through which he came to the attention of Alderman (and later sheriff) Jimmy O'Brien, who became his political mentor. After associating with the anti-Tweed Young Democracy, Croker broke with O'Brien in 1872, and was taken under the wing of Tammany Hall's new "reform" boss, John Kelly.

Running on the Tammany Hall slate in 1874, Croker was elected coroner, but he allegedly shot and killed an opponent in an election day brawl. Charged with murder, the subsequent trial ended with a hung jury, and he was not retried. The incident became an integral part of Croker's reputation, so that twenty years later Carl Schurz identified him as the political boss who "once distinguished himself by killing a man," which some old-fashioned people considered an objectionable feature of his career.

On June 2, 1886, as the Tammany Hall executive committee was conferring on a new boss to replace Kelly, who had died the day before, Croker strode into Kelly's office and took over the organization's reins. For the next sixteen years, Croker would serve as Tammany Hall boss, more administratively effective than Kelly, and more politically ruthless than Tweed. During the late 1880s and early 1890s, Croker consolidated Tammany's power by eliminating its rival Democratic machines, and ensured the mayoral election of Tammany lieutenants, Hugh Grant (1888, 1890) and Thomas Gilroy (1892). Croker worked toward his clearly stated goal of having all city posts from mayor to office porter filled by Tammany Hall members, who numbered 90,000 during his tenure.

In 1889, Mayor Grant appointed the Tammany boss to the lucrative office of city chamberlain, where he was responsible for all city deposits. He resigned the next year, though, and thereafter drew no salary from the city government or Tammany Hall. Only a few years earlier, Croker had been struggling financially, but now he was able to buy an expensive mansion on Fifth Avenue, invest large amounts in high-priced racehorses and real estate (in the United States, England, and Ireland), and was estimated to be worth several million dollars.

Unlike Tweed, Croker probably did not take most of his money directly from Tammany Hall graft, which was funneled into the machine's coffers. Instead, shortly after becoming boss, he established a real estate partnership, which sold land to the municipal government.

In addition, he earned handsome profits from city contracts awarded to numerous firms in which he had a financial interest. When an investigating commission asked Croker whether he was working as boss for his own "pocket," he replied, "All the time, the same as you." Croker did, however, receive shady cash in the traditional manner. Croker received bribe money from the owners of brothels, saloons, and illegal gambling dens. Other income came by way of gifts of stock from street railway and transit companies, for example. The city police were largely still under the control of Tammany Hall, and payoffs from vice protection operations also contributed to Tammany income.

Parkhurst handed off his information to public officials, such as State Senator Thomas C. Platt, resulting in several investigative committees being established in the 1890s. The most significant of these was the Lexow Committee.

In the wake of the 1893 depression the Democrats suffered election defeats and the Republicans took over in Albany. The Lexow Committee was a major New York State Senate probe into police corruption in 1894. The investigation, which took its name from the committee's chairman, State Senator Clarence Lexow, of Nyack, was the widest ranging of several such commissions empaneled during the 19th century. The testimony collected during its hearings ran to over 10,000 pages.

By September, as the voluminous details of police corruption were being revealed daily, the race for mayor in New York City was gearing up. It was believed that Tammany could be beaten by a fusion ticket of Republicans and anti-Tammany Democrats. William Strong was the fusion candidate and Tammany was defeated in what was seen at the time as a tremendous breakthrough in breaking Tammany's stranglehold on New York City politics. The Lexow Committee uncovered police involvement in extortion, bribery, counterfeiting, voter intimidation, election fraud, brutality, and scams.

One newspaper wrote about the hearing that it was the most detailed accounting of municipal malfeasance in history. It was discovered that the promotion of officers was largely dependent on the payment for a position, and that that payment was largely recovered from the protection of vice businesses including prostitution. Captain Timothy J. Creedon described how he paid $15,000 to obtain a captain's rank.

The Lexow Committee called some star performers from the police department to testify, such as Tommy Byrnes and Al "Clubber" Williams, but no narrative on police corruption would have been complete without the inclusion of William "Big Bill" Devery.

William Stephen Devery was born on Manhattan's East Side on Jan. 9, 1854, the oldest of the five children of Irish Catholic immigrants. Support for Tammany Hall ran in the family. Years afterward, Bill would boast that as a boy, he had carried the dinner pail when his father, a mason, laid bricks for the Tammany Hall Wigwam clubhouse on 14th Street. A 260-pound bear of a man, Devery's adult working life began as a bartender in rough Bowery establishments. Genial and hearty with a jolly red face and a thick black mustache, Devery also reputedly made money on the side as a local bare knuckles club fighter. In 1878, the 24-year-old Devery became a cop, reportedly paying the standard $200 bribe for his appointment. Because there were no civil service exams then, anyone with money could join the force. Devery saw the $200 as an investment, knowing that he would earn the sum back and much more through graft.

Because Big Bill liked to hold seminars around the pump at 28th Street and Eighth Avenue, he was known as the philosopher of the pump. Bill believed it was the police department's duty to protect the lives and property of its citizens. In return for police protection, Devery believed the citizens should not worry about what they didn't see. His advice to cops was simple: "Hear see and say nothing. Eat, drink and pay nothing."

Through the course of his career, Devery accumulated the following disciplinary record

- Oct. 25, 1878 Neglect to report Reprimanded
- Dec. 3, 1878 Conversation Fined 2 days
- July 22, 1879 Absent from roll call

Fined 1 day

- Nov. 11, 1879 Conversation Fined half day
- Jan. 27, 1880 Conduct unbecoming Complaint dismissed
- March 17, 1880 Neglect to report

Fined half day

- Nov. 25, 1887 Absent from desk duty Reprimand

Despite this less than stellar record, in due time, Devery advanced from patrolman to roundsman to sergeant, paying bribes for each promotion in the usual way. As he advanced in rank, Devery learned from Richard Croker, the ruthless Tammany Hall boss, to steer clear of saloons, gambling dens, brothels, off-track-betting parlors, dance halls, and other spots that paid Tammany. While serving on the force, Devery cemented relations with two power brokers: Big Tim Sullivan, the boss of the Lower East Side second in power only to Croker himself, and Frank Farrell, a Midtown saloon keeper and bookie who, in time, controlled a horse-racing stable, a succession of high-roller casinos, and more than 250 off-track betting parlors.

On Dec. 30, 1891, after 13 years on the force, Devery became a captain after paying $14,000. Put in charge of the Eldridge Street station, the center of New York's red-light district, he famously told his men: *"They tell me there's a lot of grafting going on in this precinct. They tell me that you fellows are the fiercest ever on graft. Now that's going to stop! If there's any grafting to be done, I'll do it. Leave it to me."*

Devery set up a clever system of taking graft. Rather than taking the bribes directly, people who needed to pay Devery for favors went to a tailor named Sam Meyer and ordered a suit. The cost of the suit was $1,000, which was the equivalent of $28,000 today. Big Bill would pick up the money from the tailor and pay tribute to his Tammany benefactors before stuffing the rest of the money in his pocket.

For the next several years, Devery was almost constantly under either indictment or charges for extortion, bribery, and other misconduct, but he always managed to beat the rap. Devery's exploits were one of the star attractions at the Lexow committee hearings, but when he was hauled before the committee to answer the allegations against him, Devery remembered nothing.

As a result of the information revealed during the hearings, on August 31, 1894, Devery was charged with bribery and extortion. He hid inside his home stating that he was too sick to attend his department trial. The situation reached a point where his wife refused to allow police department surgeons to enter his home to perform an examination. Accordingly, the board of commissioners proceeded with the trial without Devery's presence, and he was dismissed from the force. Devery appealed his conviction, and it was overturned with the court ordering his reinstatement to the police department. Most men in Devery's situation would have thanked their lucky stars that they had a job again, but not Big Bill Devery. Amazingly (with the help of his good friend Croker), over a very short period of time in 1898 he was promoted to inspector, deputy chief, and then to chief of police despite an outcry from anti-corruption advocates.

Unpretentious, good-humored, and brazenly corrupt, Devery was loved by the police rank and file, with whom he regularly socialized. Many of New York's citizens were also amused by their colorful, corrupt police chief. Devery's term as chief of police was perhaps the low point of honest policing in the city.

Based on the findings of the Lexow Committee Tammany was defeated in the 1894 elections with fusion candidate William L. Strong becoming mayor. Richard Croker was shaken by the activities of the Lexow Committee and the subsequent election, prompting him to leave for his European residences where he remained for three years.

It looked as if Tammany might be dead, but those looking to bury the organization had to stop digging their grave and take notice of something significant. The evidence uncovered by the Lexow Committee led to forty indictments of police officials, with many being tried and convicted. But two years after the hearings not one convicted person was in jail. Just about every appeal of a conviction was successful. Tammany was still very much alive.

New York City had not seen the last of Richard Croker and Tammany Hall. Croker returned to the city after his three-year European hiatus and pulled off his greatest political success in 1897 by orchestrating the election of Robert A. Van Wyck as the first mayor of the newly consolidated Greater City of New York.

Despite the Lexow Committee and reformers like Theodore Roosevelt, New York in 1900 was a city of 3.5 million people who existed under the control of Tammany Hall. An estimated 25,000 prostitutes plied their trade in houses and on the street. Concentrated on the lower east side in the famous Tenderloin (14th to 42nd Streets – 4th to 7th Avenues) they were controlled through a system of unofficial licensing and organized payoffs administered by the procurers, pimps, madams, the police, and Tammany district leaders. The brothels usually paid graft, consisting of an initiation fee of several hundred dollars for opening the house followed by regular monthly payments directly to the local police captain's wardman or collector.

Gambling was centrally controlled by a combine or syndicate whose members were Devery, Police Commissioner John Sexton, Tammany leader John Carroll, Gambler Frank Farrell, and State Senator Timothy "Big Tim" Sullivan. These men supervised about

1,100 gambling establishments including some 400 horse betting locations, known as poolrooms, which were the largest single source of graft.[2]

The investigations and reform movements made no deep impression on the city administration, and matters went along pretty much as before. On March 9, 1900, the New York Times published a detailed statement that the sum of $3,095,000 a year was being paid by the gambling-house keepers of the city to the "Gambling House Commission," which, it said, was composed of two state senators, a representative of the pool-room proprietors, and the head of one of the city departments. This commission, the article alleged, received and passed upon applications, established the tariff to be paid by the applicants, and supervised the collections. Neither the Times article nor the subsequent grand jury that was empaneled had the slightest effect on the conduct of the city administration. In November of 1900, however, a marked change occurred. For several years certain reform societies and ecclesiastical bodies, particularly the Episcopal Church, had sought to mitigate the open flaunting of immorality in the tenement houses of a particular district on the East Side. These attempts had been resisted, not only by those living on the proceeds of this immorality, but by the police themselves; and two ministers who had complained to certain police officials had been grossly insulted.

Immediately after the Presidential election, Bishop Potter, a powerful New York City clergyman, in a stinging letter of complaint, brought the matter to the attention of Mayor Van Wyck. It was a psychologic moment for such an action, and it produced immediate results. The Committee of Fifteen, a New York City citizens' group that advocated the elimination of prostitution and gambling, was established in November 1900. Inspired by Charles Parkhurst's successful unseating of machine candidates in the 1894 election, the Fifteen swore to uncover the Tammany-tolerated vice.

Sparing no expense, the Fifteen hired a team of detectives to document the moral geography of Manhattan. From their investigators' reports, the Fifteen created a precinct-by-precinct catalog that mapped the organized toleration of prostitution and gambling in Manhattan. At the same time, they used the investigators' notarized testimony to procure illicit activity occurring in the tenement districts. [3]

Croker took notice of the work of the Fifteen and paused in his preparations for his usual trip to England long enough to give orders to put down the immorality complained of, and he appointed a Committee of Five to carry his mandate into effect, or at least some satisfactory show of doing so. He went further than this, for his orders included a general order to the lawbreakers of the city to "go slow," or in other words, to observe, until further advice from headquarters, a certain degree of moderation in their infractions of the law and their outrages upon decency.[4]

Frustrated reformers believed there was no way to stem the systematic corruption in the police department as long as it had control over the election bureau. Police brass, acting on Croker's orders, selected the polling locations, divided the city into election districts, appointed inspectors and polling clerks, had ballots and registration lists printed, and tallied votes. The police also had the authority to verify "floaters" - residents of hotels and lodging houses who for a small fee voted Tammany candidates. It did not matter whether the floaters were actually registered. Tammany Hall would provide them with the names of registered voters even if these persons were long dead.

Fortunately, the State Legislature had already taken steps to rein in Tammany Hall by establishing a Charter Revision Committee led by mayoral candidate Seth Low.

Low had a reputation for reform and honesty and had served two terms as mayor of Brooklyn. In 1897 Low's ran for mayor of consolidated New York but was unsuccessful, partially because of a division among anti-Tammany Hall candidates and parties. However, four years later, he would run again with very different results.

In December 1900, Governor Theodore Roosevelt, in one of his final acts before leaving to become vice president, signed the committee's recommendations into law. The revised charter removed the Board of Elections from police department control and dissolved both the four member police board and the position of chief of police. Their powers were consolidated into a new one person police commissioner.

As a result of these changes, a new police commissioner had to be appointed. John Sexton and Bernard York, who were commissioners on the police board, sought to become police commissioner. While both men had proved to be loyal Tammany soldiers, each on occasion had exhibited an independent streak that in Croker's opinion, made them less than ideal candidates to head the police department. In addition, York was a Brooklyn native, and Croker felt he would always be loyal to the Willoughby Street political machine first. There were many other names floated as candidates, but whoever was to become the first solo police commissioner in New York City would be assuming command at a time of systematic corruption and political turmoil.

On February 23, 1901, Mayor Van Wyck appointed an unlikely candidate named Michael C. Murphy as the first single-headed police commissioner in the City of New York. Here is where our story begins.

Chapter 1: Who was Michael Murphy?

Michael Cotter Murphy was born on March 7, 1839 in Kilmallock, County Limerick, Ireland. The family emigrated to New York in 1848 and young Michael attended the public schools in the old First Ward, near the Battery and made his home in that area. After knocking around finding employment here and there young Murphy got a position in the composing room of the New York Express newspaper, and he remained in this position until the outbreak of the Civil War.

When the future police commissioner was only an 18-year-old boy setting type in the composing room for five years, he decided that there was little, if any future for him in this vocation. Thus, it happened one night after he had finished his work, that he said to a companion, "They say a printer sticks type. Do you know there's too much truth in that for me."

"How's that?" asked the companion.

"A printer is likely to stick himself. He will sit all his life on a stool. I'm going into politics, and I've already landed a job. 'General' Dan Sickles got it for me. I'm going to be night porter in the customs service."

Dan Sickles was a politician and eventual Civil War hero who was tried and acquitted for killing his wife's lover in 1859. Murphy met Sickles after his trial when Sickles was a United States Congressman.

Some weeks afterward, when he was asked why he preferred a night portership, when everyone else wanted to work during the day, he said, "I've worked in the printing business so long after dark and I can't see until after six o'clock." [5]

In researching 19th century sources of information for the Police in New York City series I found that facts contained in some of these sources, particularly the newspapers, were sometimes "fluid." Sometimes, a fact appearing in print was directly contradicted by several other sources. On face value, some of the information I found printed in the newspapers of the day seemed to be outlandish, so I learned not to include these "facts" unless I found the same information in more than one source. Michael Murphy was a prime example of this phenomenon of contradictory facts. Murphy was born in 1839, yet I found several sources that indicated his year of birth was 1841. There is very little mention of Murphy's family members, but one information source related that his parents died in Ireland and that Murphy was an orphan when he entered the United States. Additionally, a man by the name of Frank L. Bacon was listed in different newspapers as being Murphy's friend, roommate, caregiver, brother-in-law, and nephew. It was therefore, with some trepidation that I discovered a strange story regarding the short time Murphy spent working as a custodian at the Custom's House. I hesitated to include the story as part of Murphy's biography until I found the story in more than one source, which I did.

On February 22, 1860, Murphy was arrested by Captain Dowling of the Sixth Precinct for the theft of a package of watch cases valued at $1,600 from the Customs House. The owners of the property went to the station house and had a long talk with Murphy in the presence of Captain Dowling. Murphy admitted to the theft and expressed a desire to make restitution. The property owners requested that Murphy be released, stating that they would be responsible for his future appearances. With this assurance, Captain Dowling released him. The following morning, however, a warrant was issued by Justice Brennan for Murphy's arrest for a different theft of $255 worth of jewelry from the seizure room. [6]

Murphy spent two months in jail before being bailed out and enlisting in the Union Army at the outbreak of the Civil War. When the war was over and he settled back in New York City to begin a political career as a loyal soldier of Tammany Hall, the indictment that still existed for the Custom house thefts was a dark spot on his record that could potentially be a severe liability for his political aspirations.

But the powers at Tammany liked the young war veteran, and miraculously, the indictment was dismissed.

At the outbreak of the Civil War Murphy was commissioned as a Captain of the 11th New York Volunteer Infantry Regiment in May 1861 and served with the regiment until transferring to the 170th New York Infantry Regiment in July 1862 and was promoted to Lieutenant Colonel in February 1863.

As I found with several aspects of Murphy's personal life, there was a bit of confusion and controversy regarding his military record. What is certain is that for actions he took while commanding his regiment during the Battle of North Anna, Virginia, on May 24, 1864, he was awarded the Medal of Honor on January 15, 1897. His Medal of Honor citation reads: "This officer, commanding the regiment, kept it on the field exposed to the fire of the enemy for three hours without being able to fire one shot in return because of the ammunition being exhausted."

While the Medal of Honor is now the highest military decoration attainable by a member of the United States armed forces, during the Civil War, it was the only one. Thus, it was often awarded for reasons that would not now satisfy the stringent modern criteria. For example, Secretary of War Edwin M. Stanton promised a Medal of Honor to every man in the 27th Maine Volunteer Infantry Regiment who extended his enlistment.

Another intriguing question was why Murphy's Medal of Honor was awarded 33-years after the action. In reality, the extended time between the battle and the award was not that odd. It was common for Civil War Medals of Honor to be awarded decades after the conflict ended and in one case, Andrew Jackson Smith's Medal was not awarded until 2001, 137 years after the action in which he earned it. Smith's wait, caused by a missing battle report, was the longest delay of the award for any recipient, until November 6, 2014, when President Obama awarded the Medal of Honor to Union Army First Lieutenant

Alonzo Cushing for his actions at the Battle of Gettysburg, taking the longest delay of the award to 151 years. In Murphy's case, why was there a 33-year wait to receive the medal? While there is no certain answer to this question, it certainly was an asset for an up-and-coming Tammany politician to be a certified war hero.

Now we come to the confusing part of his military service. In some biographies it is stated that Murphy was dismissed from the Army in 1866 due to a disability. But there is also documentation reflecting that during the 1864 Battle of North Anna, the same engagement for which Murphy received the Medal of Honor in 1897, Colonel Murphy sent out a flag of truce during a lull in the fighting in order to bring the wounded and dying off the field. The cries of the wounded could easily be heard but Murphy could not order his men to retrieve the casualties until he had sent the flag of truce. This tactic was judged by General George Meade to be against military regulations, and he dismissed Murphy from the service. This took place while Murphy was in command of the advance line of the Second Division of the Second Army Corps. The flag of truce was sent to the skirmishing line of the enemy, in an effort to save the lives of over a hundred men and officers lying wounded between lines.

Shortly thereafter, General Ulysses S. Grant reviewed the incident and reversed Meade's decision, but it was too late. The order had been approved by the Secretary of War, and two days later, while fighting at the head of his regiment, Colonel Murphy received the order that he was dismissed. Murphy was subsequently reappointed by the governor of New York, but the regiment was then so few in number that he was never again mustered into duty.[7]

Murphy's service in the Unites States Army might have concluded, but not his military service. 1866 found him appointed a general in the Fenian Army.

The Fenian Brotherhood was an Irish Republican organization founded in the United States in 1858 with the goal of establishing

Ireland as an independent country, free from British rule. After the collapse of the 1848 Irish Rebellion James Stephens and John O'Mahony fled to Paris to avoid arrest. There, they supported themselves by teaching and translation work and planned the next stage of "the fight to overthrow British rule in Ireland." In 1856 O'Mahony went to America and founded the Fenian Brotherhood. Stephens returned to Ireland and in Dublin on St. Patrick's Day 1858, following an organizing tour through the length and breadth of the country, founded the Irish counterpart of the American Fenians, the Irish Republican Brotherhood.

Large quantities of arms were purchased, and preparations were openly made by the American Fenians for a coordinated series of raids into Canada. The end of the American Civil War proved to be the ideal time to execute these raids. The vast majority of the Fenian Army was comprised of battle-hardened veterans of the Union Army who already were functioning as cohesive military units since they had served in ethnic Irish Brigades during the war. Additionally, the United States government took no major steps to prevent the raids. Many in the U.S. administration were not indisposed to the movement because of Britain's actions of what was construed as assisting the Confederacy during the Civil War. The purpose of these raids was to seize the transportation network of Canada, with the idea that this would force the British to exchange Ireland's freedom for possession of their Province of Canada.

On May 31, 1866, the Fenians briefly captured Fort Erie, defeating a Canadian force at Ridgeway. This was the high point of the raid, for in the end, the invasion was broken by the US authorities' subsequent interruption of Fenian supply lines across the Niagara River and the arrests of Fenian reinforcements attempting to cross the river into Canada. Even without the U.S. intervention it was unlikely that such a small force would have ever achieved their goal.

General Michael Murphy had spent time recruiting for the Fenian Army in Manhattan before being dispatched to Malone, New York to prepare for a raid on Montreal. The raid never occurred because on June 7, 1866, Murphy and other Fenian officers were arrested by U.S. authorities in Malone. After his arrest, Murphy was allowed two hours to inform his men of the situation and to advise them to return home. To facilitate this movement, the U.S. government purchased rail tickets for the Fenians to return to their homes if they would promise not to invade any more countries from the United States. Murphy was kept in custody for several weeks before being released and returning to New York City. That was the end of his military career with any army.[8]

In 1866 Colonel Murphy returned to New York and settled near the Battery, and as he was a handsome young Irishman of combative habits but good natured always, he rose to be a political power in the district. Murphy took an interest in politics and became a loyal soldier for Tammany Hall and a good friend to Richard Croker, who would become the Tammany boss. He was elected to New York County's First District and served in the New York State Assembly from 1867 to 1870.

Colonel Michael C. Murphy was known at different times of his life as Commissioner Murphy, Senator Murphy, Assemblyman Murphy, Boss Murphy, Diamond Mike, and Mike the printer's devil as he evolved from an Irish immigrant into a Tammany politician. The majority of Tammany politicians held office some of the time, but usually were in and out of politics during their careers. Colonel Murphy, however, in fair and foul weather, generally managed to stay in office except for times when poor health did not permit him.

There was one other time in 1870 that Murphy's political career was derailed by a very messy episode in his personal life. A few years before Murphy left to fight in the Civil War, he fell in love with a young girl named Mary Drennan. According to Mary's uncle, John Berrigan, his niece was a 17-year-old beauty who was the belle of the ward.

Berrigan said that Murphy and Mary were married by a Catholic priest and that the entire neighborhood knew about the marriage. The couple lived in Berrigan's home at 20 Desdrosses Street until they moved into their own home on Watts Street. Berrigan said they had two children, a boy who died at age 8, and a girl who died at age 6.

Berrigan said that Murphy and Mary appeared to be happy until the Spring of 1870 when Murphy was away in Albany performing his duties with the Assembly. A priest came down from Albany and asked Berrigan and Mary if Murphy had been married before. They found the question strange, but they were shocked when the priest told them that Murphy had just married a woman named Kate Fay in Albany. Murphy came back to the city several days later and initially denied the marriage to Fay, but finally admitted to it. He then brought his second wife down to Manhattan and set her up in an apartment at 74 Varick Street.

Murphy offered to provide for his wife, Mary, but she left the Watts Street home and moved uptown. She said she was a good Catholic girl and didn't believe in divorce, and that she would not cause any trouble for Murphy. Mary's brother, John, however, when he learned of the situation, said he did intend to cause trouble. In fact, he said he was going to kill Murphy. John learned of the situation while traveling back from China. When Murphy heard about John's threat he was petrified, but John could never carry out his threat because he died in San Francisco before he could get back to New York.

Berrigan said that the second wife had money, and Murphy married her because he was broke and needed to get back on his feet financially. Kate lived with Murphy at Varick Street for seven years before she divorced him and married a man named Clements. Berrigan said that Murphy didn't dare run for the assembly again immediately after the news of his two wives got out. He kept a low profile for several years and after his second wife left him, he got back into politics because he believed his messy marriage situation would be too much a case of ancient history to hurt him. [9]

Murphy was right because he returned to the State Assembly for three years from 1881 to 1883. He then went on to serve in the 5th District New York State Senate from 1884 to 1889, sitting in the 107th, 108th, 109th, 110th, 111th and 112th New York State Legislatures.

In 1889 Murphy began experiencing stomach problems that he believed was nothing more than indigestion. Afterall, who wouldn't have developed indigestion after the tumultuous marital times he had experienced. The condition worsened, however, to the point where he could no longer swallow food. He was diagnosed with a rare gastronomical disorder that was literally causing him to waste away.

The malady reduced him from a strong, robust man of 225 pounds to a skeleton weighing 88 pounds. Doctors said an ulcer had formed on the passage to his stomach and in a few days, he would starve to death.

In a desperate attempt to save his life, Dr. RF Weir and Dr. J, Julio Henna performed a remarkable operation in which the surgeons inserted a silver metal tube directly into his stomach through which small amounts of food could be passed. At regular intervals each day liquid food was passed into his stomach through the tube. The operation was a success and Murphy slowly gained strength to the point where he could perform normal work activities, but he was never able to eat solid food again.

By 1897 Murphy's condition had slightly improved. One day he took some water into his mouth and let it run down his throat to relieve his thirst. To his surprise, he swallowed the water. He took another drink and was delighted at the sensation of swallowing, which he had not experienced in years. Since that time, he was able to swallow some coffee and very small amounts of food. Still, his condition had taken a terrible toll on him. At one time Murphy weighed over 240 pounds, but his affliction had caused his weight to drop to 130 pounds. [10]

Despite his deteriorating physical condition, Murphy was still a loyal friend to Richard Croker, and when Croker made his stunning comeback with Robert Van Wyck's victory in the 1897 mayoral election, Murphy's loyalty would be rewarded. On March 3, 1898, Murphy was appointed by Mayor Van Wyck as Commissioner of Health of the City of New York.

Chapter 2: The Appointment

Theodore Roosevelt, in one of his final acts as Governor of New York before becoming Vice President of the United States in March 1901, continued the reforms he began when he was a police commissioner by signing legislation that replaced the police board and office of the police chief with a single police commissioner. Roosevelt then passed the torch of police reform to the next governor, Benjamin Odell.

In 1894, Odell was elected as a Republican to the 54th United States Congress, serving New York's 17th Congressional District. He ran for, and was reelected in 1896, but declined to run in 1898. He became one of the most powerful New York Republican operatives of his time, serving for ten years as chairman of the Republican State Executive Committee, both before and after his two terms in Congress.

In 1898, Odell was the first to suggest to Republican boss Thomas C. Platt that Theodore Roosevelt ought to be the Republican candidate for governor, which met Platt's protest. With Platt convinced that Roosevelt was a figure who would disturb state politics, Odell used his position as the Republicans' state chairman to convince Platt that Governor Black would lose reelection if nominated in 1898. Returning as a hero from the Spanish-American War, Roosevelt's campaign, under Odell's management, would win the governorship by a comfortable margin in 1898. In his biography, then former President Roosevelt would say Odell was one of three men most responsible for his candidacy being pressed on Platt.

In the state election of 1900, Thomas C. Platt wanted to rid himself of Theodore Roosevelt from the governorship of New York. Devising a scheme to have Roosevelt nominated to replace the late Garret Hobard as Vice president to President William McKinley, Platt placed Odell as nominee for governor in 1900. Odell would go on to handily defeat John B. Stanchfield in the general election to succeed Theodore Roosevelt as Governor of New York.

Taking office on January 1, 1901, one of the first items on Odell's agenda was to see that Roosevelt's police bill was enacted into law. The new police bill seemed to be bad news for Big Bill Devery because it eliminated the position of chief of police.

Governor Odell summed up the situation: "*There is no necessity, it seems to me, for a commissioner who is not in effect as well as in name the absolute head of the police system of the City of New York. An efficient man as the single-headed commissioner with all the power now possessed by the Chief of Police, would at once narrow down the responsibility and place it within the responsibility of the chief executive of the state to hold accountable the mayor and the commissioner thus appointed. This suggestion, if passed by the legislature, would, in my opinion, be no violation of the principle of home rule. It is moreover, right, that inasmuch as the governor is equally responsible, he should have an authority over the department, because the people, not only of New York City, but of the whole state, are interested, and certain powers only to be exercised in emergencies should be conferred upon him to enable him to carry out the constitutional mandates. I recommend, therefore, the substitution of a single headed police commissioner for the City of New York, such commissioner to be the chief of police of the city, to be appointed by the mayor and subject to removal by either the mayor or the governor, and that the present office of a separate chief of police be abolished.*"

The governor laid out the message clearly for Devery. His position was being legislated away, and Mayor Van Wyck and Tammany would not have the nerve to appoint Devery as police commissioner because Governor Odell would promptly remove him from office. The police bill not only replaced the police board and its four commissioners with one police commissioner, but it also gave the governor the authority to remove the police commissioner from office, but the successor could only be appointed by the mayor. [11]

Members of the police department from the highest officials to the patrolmen on the beat wanted to talk about nothing but the police bill. Rumors, many of which were absurd, were flying thick and fast. They related to the constitutionality of the new bill, to the fate of Chief Devery and some of the other officials to be legislated out of office by the bill. The conversations also involved what action the mayor would take when the bill had been passed by the Legislature and to the choice of the new commissioner of police if the bill became a law. Police officials large and small seemed to be imbued with the idea that the new police commissioner, who would have all the powers now held by the police board and the chief of police for the enforcement of the law and the discipline of the force, would be "the biggest official in the whole city." Some of the policemen said that they thought there should be an amendment to the bill, changing the title of the police head from "Commissioner" to "Czar."

It was evident from the talk of policemen who had not risen from the ranks that they looked with fear and trembling for the coming of an absolute ruler of the force who would serve out swift justice to those who shirked duty or who held easy places by favor of political friends. It was also evident from the talk of some police officials that they believed the new bill would be unconstitutional if it was permitted to retain the provision for the summary removal of the commissioner by the governor without charges. There were many rumors in police and political circles as to the action of Mayor Van Wyck when the police bill was passed. Many of the politicians said that they believed the mayor would veto the bill, declaring that it was unconstitutional. If the bill became a law, however, he would be expected to appoint "some good Democrat." [12]

Very quickly, the guessing game began in the press regarding who would be the police commissioner. The favorite in many minds was the president of the current four-man police board, Bernard York. But in the opinion of close observers of the political game, it was thought that some entirely new man would get the position. Since Croker knew that the new police bill would give the governor the power to remove the police commissioner, it would not be the wisest choice to select an obvious Tammany pawn. He might be better off with a compromise between a Tammany man and a real reformer. He was really going to have to "thread the needle" to come up with a commissioner who would be acceptable to the reformers, but still do Tammany's bidding. [13]

During early January of 1901 names began to fly around political circles and the newspapers identifying the favorites to be selected as the single-headed police commissioner. James J. Martin was president of the police board at the time of the Lexow revelations, but he had not been conspicuous politically of late. John I. Scannell, who was the current fire commissioner, was one of Croker's closest friends, and was reputed to be extremely wealthy, always an attraction for Tammany appointments. John Y. Keller was the commissioner of charities and had been conspicuous in the news for his investigation of abuses at Bellevue Hospital. John B. Sexton was the pure Tammany representative on the present police board. If he was at all opposed to the vice system, he had concealed his feelings. Bernard J. York, president of the police board, represented Brooklyn and a loathing for Chief Devery. Politicians had no great faith in his chance of becoming the sole police commissioner. Lewis Nixon was the East River Bridge Commissioner and had recently been pushed into prominence as the active head of Tammany's Vice Committee of Five. He was supposed to be groomed for the Tammany nomination for mayor. Thomas Byrnes was chief of police at the time of the Lexow committee disclosures, but was retired when the Strong administration came into power. John Fox was the president of the Democratic Club and an ex-state senator who also had no use for Devery. [14]

Regardless of the final choice for police commissioner, it was clear to everyone, including Bill Devery, that one of the goals of the police bill and the elimination of the chief of police position, was to remove Devery from the force. This left Devery with a conundrum because he was not eligible for retirement on a pension upon his own application. This was likely the reason that explained why Devery refused to listen to the persuasive eloquence of members of the Tammany Committee of Five and others who had suggested his voluntary and graceful retirement from office as the noose of evidence against him continued to tighten. The provision of law for the retirement of a policeman at that time was explicit. A policeman who had reached the age fifty-five years and had served twenty years on the force could be retired upon his own application or upon a certificate by the surgeons that he was not able to perform police duty. A policeman who had served twenty-five years on the force must be retired upon his own application provided there were no charges pending against him. Devery had not been a policeman twenty-five years, and he was not fifty-five years old. He was too strong and robust to permit the issue of a surgeon's certificate of unfitness for police duty.

Devery became a policeman on June 19, 1878, and with the time he was off the department due to his dismissal, he had a term of service of only twenty-two years and six months. He was born in 1854 and was not much over forty-six years old. He would be unable, therefore, to force his retirement on a pension by making application for retirement. There was a special provision in the charter by which a chief of police could be retired, without his own application, by the unanimous vote of the commissioners, or by the votes of three commissioners and the vote of the mayor. It was under that provision that John McCullagh was retired from the office of chief of police, to make room for Devery. Well informed police officials said that Devery was not to be retired, but if it became certain that the Legislature would pass a bill to legislate him out of office, there was a chance his friends on the Police Board may vote to give him a retiring pension. [15]

By January 10th the specific language in the police bill was printed in the newspapers:

Section 1. The terms of office of the Police Commissioners of the city of New York heretofore constituting the Police Board shall cease and determine within ten days after the passage of this act, and the powers, duties and functions now by law exercised by and imposed on them, are hereby granted to and concentrated upon and vested in a single Police Commissioner, who shall be appointed by the Mayor of said city within ten days after the passage of this act.

Sec. 2. The said Commissioner shall, unless sooner removed, hold office for the term of five years and until his successor shall be appointed and has qualified. During his term of office, the said Commissioner may whenever in the judgment of the Mayor of said city or the Governor the public interests shall so require, be removed from office by either. The successors in office of the said Commissioner shall also be appointed by the Mayor of the city and shall be removed by either the Mayor or Governor whenever the public interests so require.

Sec. 3. The office of Chief of Police In the city of New York is hereby abolished, and the powers, duties and functions now by law exercised by and imposed on said Chief of Police are hereby granted to, concentrated upon and vested in the said Police Commissioner.

Sec. 4. The said Commissioner shall have the power to appoint from the citizens of the United States and residents or the said city, and at pleasure remove, two deputies, to be known as First Deputy Commissioner and Second Deputy Commissioner. The First Deputy Commissioner shall, during the absence or disability of the Commissioner, possess all the powers and perform all the duties of the Commissioner except the power of making appointments and transfers. In the absence or disability of both the Commissioner and the First Deputy Commissioner the Second Deputy Commissioner shall possess all the powers and perform all the duties of the Commissioner except the power of making appointments and transfers. The Commissioner shall define the duties of the Deputy Commissioners and may delegate to either of them any of his powers except the power of making appointments and transfers.

Sec. 5. The said Commissioner shall, from and after the passage of this act, have no cognizance of or control over the general Bureau of Elections and its branches, and the said Bureau of Elections and its branches shall no longer be a part of the said Police Department and are hereby abolished.

Sec. 6. The fiscal officer of the Police Department shall be the Controller of the City of New York, who is hereby vested with all the powers and functions heretofore existing in the treasurer of the Police Board.

Sec. 7. Nothing contained in this act shall be construed to repeal any statute of the State or ordinance of the City of New York not inconsistent with the provisions of this act, and the same shall remain in full force and effect when not inconsistent with the provisions of this act, and shall be construed and enforced in harmony with the provisions of this act. All acts and parts of acts inconsistent with the provisions of this act are hereby repealed.

Brooklyn was a key player in this process. In 1898 the City of Brooklyn had been consolidated into the Greater City of New York, with the Brooklyn Police Department becoming part of the New York City Police Department. In those early years after consolidation, however, the merger of the Brooklyn and New York Police Departments was mostly on paper. For the most part, the Brooklyn force continued to be an independent entity. The Brooklyn political machine at Willoughby Street had great interest in the upcoming police appointments. Assemblyman McKeown, head of the Kings County Democratic delegation, and popularly known as the "Brooklyn Watchdog." was asked why he could smile with only forty-five Democrats in the Assembly?

"Well," McKeown said, "these Republicans are not so bad after all. They have a police bill which some of them think we are going to fight and stir up a lot of talk. They're mistaken, that's all. I do not know the opinion of all the Democrats from Kings County, but I know my own views, and am inclined to think the rest are something of the same mind. Now. Personally, I am in favor of a single headed police commissioner. The police system of the city of Brooklyn before consolidation had a single head, and we got along on the east side of the East River very well indeed. At any rate, we did not have all the trouble that is now going on over the Police Department, with the charges against it of blackmail and a lot of other sins."

The Brooklyn politicians and police officials also had no love for Big Bill Devery, so they were not going to stand in the way of any bill that would legislate him out of the police department.[16]

Richard Croker was still trying to decide who to tell the mayor to appoint as police commissioner when an interesting event occurred that may have swayed his decision.

Henry Codman Potter was a bishop of the Episcopal Church of the United States, and he was the seventh bishop of the Episcopal Diocese of New York. Potter was a respected and influential force in the city, with an official once referring to him as " a man more praised and appreciated, perhaps, than any public man in New York City's long list of great citizens."

The fallout from Bishop Potter's previous complaint to the mayor was fresh in Croker's memory. Rev. Robert L. Paddock had reported vice in his area to the police, and instead of taking action they insulted Paddock. This affront led to the formation of the Committee of Fifteen to investigate vice in the city, and to the necessity for Croker to establish his own Committee of Five, to at least make it look like Tammany was taking the vice situation in the city seriously. [17]

When Bishop Potter spoke, Croker listened, and as the decision on a police commissioner drew near, Bishop Potter entered into the discussions by expressing the opinion that the head of the police department should be a man with military training. The Bishop said in response to an inquiry that he thought the plan of placing an Army officer at the head of the force was to be commended.

"The plan worked well in London," Potter said. "If an Army officer in active service could not be obtained for the position of police commissioner a retired officer of large experience, with a good record and in good health, would meet the requirements.

Meanwhile, the rumors regarding Devery's fate were still running rampant. There were renewed reports coming out of police headquarters on January 13th that the chief of police would be retired soon. One report was that the chief was to be retired as early as the next day. That report proved to be false and Devery refused to talk on the subject. President York of the police board declined to say anything at all regarding Devery. Another commissioner said he did not think Devery could be retired at present. It was believed by some of the officials in the department that President York wanted to keep Devery in office until he was legislated out by the new police law. Then Devery would not receive a pension. It was admitted that Devery was not eligible for retirement on his own application, and the only way he could receive a pension would be by the unanimous vote of the commissioners or by the votes of three commissioners and the mayor.

As the fate of his job and pension were still very much in jeopardy, Big Bill had more immediate concerns. It was expected he would be in a bad situation when he was called to the witness chair in the Herlihy trial. The indictment accused Captain Herlihy, the commanding officer of the Twelfth Precinct of willfully failing to take action against establishments within the precinct that he knew were committing criminal violations. Devery was sure to be asked if he had been requested by Herlihy to issue warrants for the forcible entry of some the establishments in Herlihy's precinct. If he admitted that he was informed by Herlihy of the existence of certain illegal places and did not give warrants, it would be a cause for proceeding against Devery himself, while if he said the captain never gave him information to require the warrants, the fate of Herlihy would be sealed. [18]

Devery took the witness stand wearing civilian clothes and he appeared to be ill at ease. Almost immediately he was asked if Captain Herlihy ever reported to him that he had good grounds to believe that any house within the Twelfth Precinct was being used for lewd or obscene purposes.

Herlihy's attorney, Mr. Grant, jumped up. "Don't answer that question," he shouted to Devery.

The objection was overruled and Commissioner York, who was presiding over the trial, directed Devery to answer the question.

"In my experience with the police department," Devery began.

"Forget about your experience," York admonished, "just answer the question."

"I never received such a report." Devery responded.

Eventually, the board of commissioners voted three to one to dismiss the charges against Captain Herlihy, with York being the only guilty vote.

The Herlihy case was brought after a complaint by Bishop Potter, and it reinforced in Croker's mind not to forget about the feelings of the Bishop in making the choice for police commissioner.

On January 27th Governor Odell said that the bill abolishing the present four headed police board of New York and substituting for it a single commissioner would be passed immediately and made it clear that no further amendments to the bill would be accepted. The bill, therefore, in its present shape, would be likely to pass the Senate and Assembly when it came up for a third reading. The police bill, as finally amended, ended the terms of office of the present police commissioners of New York within ten days after it was signed by Governor Odell, and transferred their powers, duties and functions to a single police commissioner, who was to be appointed by Mayor Van Wyck within ten days after the measure was passed. The bill further said that the mayor or the governor could remove the police commissioner. The bill also struck at Devery by abolishing the office of chief of police and transferring its powers to the new police commissioner. The police commissioner would have two deputies, at salaries of $4,000 each, to whom he could delegate all his duties except those of making appointments and transfers. If it were not for the large Republican majority in both the Senate and the Assembly, the Tammany Hall leaders would have made a more resolute effort to defeat the police bill. [19]

On January 29th the State Senate passed the police bill, putting an end to the terms of the present four police commissioners of New- York City and abolishing the office of chief of police— there were 31 votes for the bill and 14 against.

The final hurdle for the bill was the vote in the Assembly. Once the Assembly passed the bill, Mayor Van Wyck was expected to retain the bill for the full fifteen days permitted him by the State Constitution before vetoing the bill. The Legislature would then pass the bill over the mayor's veto, and Governor Odell had already said that he would sign the bill as soon as it reached his desk. Mayor Van Wyck would then have ten additional days in which to appoint a police commissioner. Therefore, it would be sometime around the end of February when New York City would receive its first single-headed police commissioner. [20]

While the political posturing ran its course prior to the signing of the police bill, the big question continued to be, who would be the new police commissioner? There was a very strong belief that one of the current commissioners on the police board, John B. Sexton, would be the choice. Just when it appeared that the Sexton rumor may be true, suddenly, a new challenger appeared in the news with Lewis Nixon's name coming front and center as the likely appointee because of his close friendship with Croker.

In 1895, the New York Legislature authorized the East River Bridge Commission to undertake a second span across the river, ultimately known as the Williamsburg Bridge. In January 1898 Mayor

Van Wyck sacked the entire membership of the Commission, complaining of its slow and expensive pace. He appointed Nixon as the commission's new president. Nixon continued to serve as the commission's president during the bridge's construction until the commission's powers were transferred to the Commissioner of Bridges on January 1, 1902.

Nixon was also active in Democratic Party politics. In December 1901, Richard Croker chose Nixon as his successor. Croker's choice of Nixon surprised observers, because Nixon had spoken out against vice and corruption in city government, and seemingly had nothing in common with Croker. Nixon resigned several months later, explaining that, "I find that I cannot retain my self-respect and remain the leader of the Tammany organization." [21]

Despite the growing public sentiment that Nixon would be the police commissioner, as late as February 19th Sexton told the press that he fully expected to be appointed police commissioner.

The path of the police bill went as expected. Mayor Van Wyck vetoed the bill knowing full well that the bill would still pass in Albany and be signed by the governor. The mayor would take the full fifteen days allowed to him by law before sending it back to Albany for the governor's signature. During the waiting period while the mayor held the bill, he convened a hearing on the new police bill at City Hall that failed to bring a single person to speak in favor of or in opposition to the bill. The mayor walked out of his private office at 11 A.M. and said, "This is a hearing on Senate Bill 63 and Assembly Bill 140, an act relating to the police department of the city of New- York. Is there any one present who wishes to speak on the bill, either for or against?"

There was no answer for a moment or so, and then the mayor declared the hearing closed. The mayor gave out a letter which he had received from the City Club, opposing the bill on the grounds that it gave duplicate power to the mayor and the governor to remove the police commissioner. Enclosed with the letter was a long-printed memorandum, which closed with the statement: "What New-York needs is a police department with one man at the head for whose appointment and removal the mayor is responsible." [22]

Bishop Potter's words regarding placing a military man in charge of the police department were still ringing in Richard Croker's head when a new name surfaced as a candidate for police commissioner - Colonel Michael C Murphy, President of the Health Board.

"Is it true that you are to be the new police commissioner?" Colonel Murphy was asked.

"That's a leading question," he replied, evasively. "Well, there's not much in it," Murphy continued. "There's too many birds flying around on the lookout for that Job. I am afraid you reporters will have to take another guess." [23]

On February 22nd, while Governor Odell was affixing his signature on the bill, Mayor Van Wyck's office was silent. In fact, it was locked and empty with the mayor spending the morning and early afternoon at Tammany Hall. When word reached him that the bill had been signed, he proceeded to City Hall accompanied by Colonel Murphy, John B. Sexton, and Col. Ladd, Assistant Corporation Counsel attached to the mayor's office.

About 3 P.M. the small group entered the basement door on the Park Row side and walked noiselessly along the darkened corridor until they came to the narrow stairs leading to the main floor. They tiptoed up the stairs and along the corridor so noiselessly that the watchman, though wide awake, never heard them. The party entered the mayor's office without attracting any attention and locked the door behind them. Once inside he administered the oath of office to Col. Murphy appointing him as the first single police commissioner in New York City. Sexton, who had been one of the four commissioners on the old police board was sworn into Murphy's old job as commissioner of the Health Department. In the aftermath of the appointments Murphy seemed thrilled, but as Sexton departed to return to Police headquarters, he did not share the excitement. Right up until the time of the appointments Sexton believed he was about to be appointed police commissioner. City Hall was almost deserted, and the coming and going of people present for the swearing in ceremony would have escaped observation but for Murphy's heavy cane, which resounded on the marble.[24]

Chapter 3: Who's in Charge?

Newly appointed Police Commissioner Murphy headed to police headquarters accompanied by Col. Ladd and John M. Willis, secretary of the Tammany Hall General Committee of the First Assembly District. They arrived at police headquarters at about 4:15 P.M., about thirty minutes after the mayor's action had been telephoned to Chief of Police Devery. Murphy, Ladd and Willis went to Devery's office, where the chief was waiting with Sexton, who had beaten Murphy to headquarters. The group remained behind closed doors for thirty minutes. Finally, the office door opened and the newspaper men who had gathered in the anteroom were summoned in. Colonel Murphy shook hands with several reporters before making the following statement:

"I ought to say to you gentlemen, for the public, that all I ask is that I may be proved according to my deeds. I have been appointed New York City Police Commissioner and I declare that I am going to enforce the laws as I find them, and I do not care who may interfere or try to interfere with me, I shall carry out that program."

The huge grin Devery was wearing behind his desk supplied a hint to Murphy's next statement.

"Desiring to have with me men with as much experience as possible in police business, I have appointed William S. Devery my First Deputy Commissioner."

Devery had not been smiling when the new police commissioner entered his office thirty minutes earlier. In fact, it was determined that Devery had handed Murphy the following letter:

Colonel Michael C. Murphy, Police Commissioner

Sir: I hereby protest against being removed from my position as chief of police in the police department of the city of New York.

I claim that I am entitled to hold the said office of chief of police in the police department of the city of new York; that the act passed that removes the four commissioners and provides for a single commissioner and abolishes the office of chief of police is unconstitutional, void, and of no effect, and does not abolish said office of chief of police; that no method prescribed by law has been taken to retire or remove me from said office of chief of police or from the position which I hold in the police department, and I am therefore lawfully entitled to enjoy all the rights, powers, and privileges incident to said office and incident to my being a member of the police department of the City of New York.

In permitting you or anyone else to occupy my office or to do any act in derogation of my rights I do so under protest.

WILLIAM S. DEVERY

Chief of Police

Murphy accepted the document and then immediately informed Devery he was the new First Deputy Commissioner.

Devery refused to discuss the matter with reporters, but it was suspected that his smile wasn't completely genuine, nor was his legal battle over. No one believed Big Bill would passively accept his salary transitioning from $6,000 a year to the First Deputy Commissioner's salary of $4,000.

In Albany, when the governor received word of Murphy's appointment as police commissioner he was pleased. Odell thought well of Murphy and was inclined to believe he would make a good police commissioner. But when he heard that Devery had been retained as First Deputy Commissioner, he was outraged. He regarded Devery's appointment as an affront to himself and the Legislature. His first impulse was to utilize the power he wielded in the new police bill and remove Murphy from office. He quickly rejected this path because he believed Mayor Van Wyck was the driving force behind

Devery's appointment, not Murphy. If Odell utilized his legal authority to remove Murphy from office, the mayor would certainly appoint another Tammany commissioner and Devery would still be in office. The governor was going to have to face the reality that he had been outmaneuvered by Tammany and that Devery was not leaving the police department. For all intents and purposes, Devery's retention had nullified the police bill legislation which was enacted to improve the conditions in the New York City Police department, with one of its primary goals being the removal of Devery.

Unhappiness to the day's proceedings was not reserved for Albany. The appointment of Colonel Murphy was a keen disappointment to Democrats in Brooklyn who had expected that Bernard J. York, the president of the outgoing four-man police board, would be appointed police commissioner. But the news that most outraged the Kings County leaders was the retention of Devery as First Deputy Commissioner. Ever since his defiance of the Willoughby Street machine by his transfer of Deputy Chief Patrick H. McLaughlin to Queens, the Brooklyn organization had held a grudge against Devery. [25]

Patrick H. McLaughlin's police career in Brooklyn spanned over forty years, and for a time, he was in command of the Brooklyn force. Although regarded as the wealthiest policeman in Brooklyn, McLaughlin always enjoyed a reputation for strict honesty, and it was generally known that he accumulated a fortune supposed to be worth more than $250,000 through close saving and fortunate speculation in real estate during a boom time in the Bedford district. McLaughlin joined the Brooklyn Police Department in 1866 and was promoted to inspector in 1886. When the consolidation of the City of Greater New York occurred in 1898, McLaughlin succeeded John Mackeller as commander of the Brooklyn force. While he was in this position Devery took a dislike to him and began referring to McLaughlin as "a fellow who goes around with a plug hat on his head." Finally, Devery transferred McLaughlin to Queens, replacing him at Brooklyn Headquarters with Elias P. Clayton. Devery made the mistake of not consulting with Brooklyn political boss Hugh McLaughlin, prompting the entire Brooklyn political machine to hold Devery in contempt from that point forward. [26]

While the Brooklyn leaders had been given no assurances about York's appointment, they were given every reason to believe that Devery's departure from the force was certain.

The word spreading through the police department was that Devery, who had run the department as chief of police, would continue calling the shots as first deputy commissioner. Anyone who thought otherwise only needed to see the new commissioner and his deputy standing next to each other. Murphy was a man of feeble health who could not endure long hours of duty at headquarters. He presented a stunning contrast next to Devery, who was a man of massive and muscular build. [27]

When Lewis Nixon read his morning papers, he was unusually angry. There was a telephone in his house and every time he answered a ring a voice came through the electric stillness, "What do you think about the appointment of Devery?"

Nixon's answer was always the same. "It's a shame and an outrage – those people are capable of anything."

Nixon was still upset when reporters tracked him down that evening and asked for a statement. "I won't say a word," he said. "I don't dare. I'd explode if I did. That's true. If I gave expression to my feelings, there would be an explosion here. These people are capable of anything."

When he reached his home at 15 West 39th Street there was a sea of reporters waiting for him, and the following exchange took place:

Q.- Mr. Nixon, has Mr, Croker endorsed or authorized the appointment of Devery?

A.- I cannot bring myself to believe that Mr. Croker has done any such thing. If Mr. Croker sent a cable permitting or endorsing the appointment of Devery, he was grossly deceived by someone.

Q.- What do you think of Devery's appointment?

A.- I think it is unwise, both from a point of competency and of policy. Under his administration the Police Department reached the most acute stage in the history of the city.

Q.- Are you going to get off the Committee of Five?

A.- Haven't made up my mind yet.

Q.- You were pretty angry this morning?

A.- Yes (laughing), that's so, but I've cooled off a little since.

Q.- Mr. Nixon, is not Mr. Murphy, the new chief, a man of strong personality – a man of force?

A.- Well, er-er, I suppose fairly so.

Q.- Will Devery dominate Murphy?

A.- I don't know, that remains to be seen.

Q.- Will you serve on Commissioner Murphy a list of the gambling houses and disorderly houses such as you served on his predecessors?

A.- The District Attorney has them already.

Q.- Don't you consider it strange that a man familiar with all the testimony against the police which has been placed in the hands of the District Attorney should accept a position where he is likely to nullify the evidence?

A.- Why don't you write that out. I can't answer such a long question.

Q.- Mr. Murphy's appointment was urged by the Committee of Five, was it not?

A. I did not consult with anyone about it.

Q. Commissioner, the other day you said the committee was a unit in its desire to find the man in the police department responsible for the great prevalence of vice. Your committee practically accused Devery of being the man. Now, one of your committee appoints Devery deputy commissioner, and you and your associates on the committee are both angry and shocked.

The impression prevails that there was treachery on the part of either Mayor Van Wyck, Commissioner Murphy or Mr. Croker. Was there any treachery?

A.- You have outlined the situation beautifully, but I can't answer your question tonight.

The reality of the situation was that there were only two possible reasons for Murphy's action. He was either being obedient to the wishes of Van Wyck, and/or Croker, or he was guilty of one of the blackest pieces of political treachery on record.

Several weeks earlier, the Committee of Five, which consisted of Nixon, Keller, Claussen, M. Warley Platzek, and Murphy, discovered that Chief Devery was the man around which revolved the Tammany system of protected vice. At that time, they issued a statement in which they publicly declared that Devery was responsible for the existence of gambling houses and pool-rooms in the city, and that he could close them all within 48-hours if he desired.

As the time drew near for the police bill to become law, the Committee of Five discussed candidates, and Keller, Platzek, and Claussen suggested that Mayor Van Wyck be urged to appoint Commissioner Murphy, one of their own number. Nixon dissented mildly, but the others went ahead and spoke to the mayor.

Before his name was suggested to the mayor, Murphy had been particularly vocal on the unfitness of Devery, and the others on the committee confirmed that Murphy spoke strongly against Devery and gave them to understand that Devery would be run out of the department as soon as possible.[28]

There was a general belief among the police and the politicians that so long as Tammany Hall retained control of the mayor's office, Devery would remain the real master of the police force. No matter how many times the governor removed the police commissioner, every new commissioner appointed by the mayor would be pledged to keep Devery in command.

A source inside the mayor's office said that when Van Wyck called Murphy to City Hall to appoint him as police commissioner, Murphy wanted to name former Chief of Police Tommy Byrnes, who was a close friend, but that Van Wyck would not make the appointment until Murphy agreed to appoint Devery, the man who Van Wyck called the best police chief New York ever had.[29]

On Murphy's second day on the job the rumor was spreading that he was set to appoint Deputy Chief McLaughlin, of Brooklyn, as his second deputy commissioner. It was noticed, however, that McLaughlin was not at police headquarters to greet Murphy. When the commissioner consented to talk with the newspaper men he was asked if he still intended to appoint McLaughlin to the office of second deputy commissioner.

"I can't say right now," Murphy replied. "A man's mind changes very often."

The questioning continued. "If McLaughlin were here now, would you offer him the appointment?"

"But he isn't," Murphy snapped, "and I can't answer hypothetical questions."

"Well, commissioner," a reporter followed up, "will there be another deputy commissioner at all?"

"Oh, yes," Murphy nodded. "There will be two deputy commissioners. I can assure you of that, and it is safe to say that one of them will be from Brooklyn." [30]

It was never Croker's intention to have Murphy forsake his precarious health to devote himself entirely to the department. Croker was shrewd enough to realize that there was too much money at stake to let a novice take complete charge of the force, so just like the police board, the new police commissioner received his marching orders straight from the Tammany Hall sachem.

As soon as Murphy settled into the large second floor office at 300 Mulberry Street, one that had been previously occupied by the four members of the police board, he sought to justify his appointment of Devery as first deputy commissioner. Murphy explained that it was his desire to have men with as much experience as was possible in the police business with him. For the record, Devery accepted the position under protest because he felt that actions by the Charter Revisions Committee to abolish the police board and the chief of police position were illegal. There was also a monetary consideration. As first deputy commissioner, he was paid $2,000 per year less than as chief of police.

Reformers who had hoped to get rid of Devery by eliminating his position found little solace in the fact that he had accepted a pay cut to become second in command of the police force. This overt act of sedition by Murphy to circumvent the principal intention of the Charter Revision Committee outraged state Republicans, as well as a number of Tammany Hall Democrats who had sought to clean up the department. But nothing came of their protests. Meanwhile, Colonel Murphy settled into his job by deferring most of the important decisions to his second in command. In his new post Devery also acted as trial commissioner, a responsibility that had previously fallen under the purview of the police board. Every Thursday morning, patrolmen who had received charges during the previous week traveled to headquarters to face the Big Chief, as he was still referred to by the rank and file.

Devery sat behind a large horseshoe – shaped desk. Patrolmen sat stoically before him in wooden pews, dressed in starched blue uniforms with polished brass buttons, waiting for their cases to be called. Oddly enough, officers who attempted to perform their sworn duty fared no better than those who shirked their responsibility. When a patrolman appeared before Devery, sporting a deep cut over his temple, the result of a fierce struggle with a suspect who had managed to escape despite being fired at by the officer, Devery ordered a fine of twenty-days pay for not hittin' him.

The harsh sentences meted out by Devery and the iron fist with which he ruled the department continued to undermine police morale to the point that his actions got Croker's attention. If Tammany Hall was going to secure the patrolmen's vote in the 1901 mayoral election, something had to be done other than threatening them with constant transfers.

Republicans sought to garner votes from the unhappy officers by proposing legislature for a three-platoon duty system with daily eight-hour shifts and fewer hours on reserve, long sought by the Patrolmen's Benevolent Association. The Van Wyck administration resisted at first because it estimated that $2.5 million would have to be added to the department budget. But money was no object for Tammany Hall when votes were at stake. The new schedule went into effect on August 13, 1901. [31]

Murphy met with all the members of the force at the rank of captain and above and asserted that he was the real head of the police department. As soon as the meeting was over, however, he issued an order giving First Deputy Commissioner Devery all the powers of the former chief of police title. [32]

Murphy directed all his captains to forward to him reports identifying all locations in their precincts of illegal gambling, poolrooms, and other illegal activities. A reporter was present in his office when the reports were received. The reporter asked Murphy what action he would take against these locations. Murphy shrugged and said that once he went through the reports, he very well may find that there were no illegal locations operating in the city. [33]

There were questions as to whether Murphy's frail physical condition would be able to withstand the rigors of his new job. After all, he was loaded with duties and responsibilities that were formerly performed by four men, and he had also entered an entirely new field of administration, surrounded by a body of subordinates he hardly knew.

But as his first week on the job drew to a close, Murphy's stock of wiry vitality seemed far from depleted. [34]

Commissioner Murphy addressed the issue of who was in charge of the department with a mantra that would come to be looked upon as comical by some observers. "I alone am the responsible head of the police force of New York City and as such I shall see that the law is enforced, I shall in no wise countenance any violations that are brought to my attention, no matter what influence behind them, and I shall depend upon the people of New York to aid me in making the city law abiding and safe for moral and material welfare. Complaints made directly to me will be at once acted upon. Of course, it may be that I might be deceived by a subordinate. It might happen once but never again."

The statement was made to a reporter, who noted that this man with vast power over 8000 police officers weighed scarcely 90-pounds and whose body was feeble, but whose mind was vigorous and alert. When he was sworn in Murphy was 62-years-old. His eyes were cold grey, and his voice, while weak, was distinct. [35]

On March 3rd, Murphy named Bernard York, the former president of the police board, second deputy commissioner. While Murphy made the appointment, it was an agreement between Tammany Hall and the Willoughby Street Brooklyn political machine that sealed the deal. The Brooklyn organization submitted York's name only after Tammany agreed that the second deputy commissioner would have complete authority over the police in Brooklyn and Queens. It was not surprising that Tammany would acquiesce to this demand. Even though it had been over three years since the Brooklyn Police Department had been consolidated into the Greater City of New York, for the most part, not much had changed and the police in Brooklyn were still treated as their own separate entity.

Willoughby Street was not happy when Devery was retained as first deputy commissioner and they wanted assurances that Devery would not be interfering with operations in Brooklyn. That assurance alone was not enough to sway York, who indicated he was finished with the policing business and wanted no part of the job, with or without Devery's interference. Ultimately, however, York was a loyal soldier of the Brooklyn machine, and since he had future aspirations to be appointed as a judge, he finally agreed to accept the appointment. [36]

Murphy truly was between a rock and a hard place. Public opinion had swung heavily against Tammany due to the well-publicized corruption that was being tolerated and approved by the police department. Croker knew the elections in November could be a disaster for Tammany, so he needed Murphy to clamp down on the rampant vice in the city – but not too much. Too many Tammany politicians like himself made huge sums of money from these illegal activities. [37]

Very quickly Murphy was forced to walk back his statement asserting that there were no gambling houses open in the city. The Society for the Prevention of Crime was formed in 1878 for the purpose of exposing illegal activity in the city and the associated police corruption. This organization did more than just complain to deaf ears at Tammany Hall and Police Headquarters.

43 Mercer Street was located within the district where Murphy resided for years. Mr. Burr, the superintendent of the SPC engaged private detectives to watch the location for several days, and after observing evidence of illegal gambling at the site, Mr. Burr appeared before Supreme Court Justice William Jerome and was granted a warrant for the location. Armed with the warrant, Burr, accompanied by several private detectives and Justice Jerome entered the MacDougal Street police station and showed the warrant to a stunned Captain Albertson. At the direction of Justice Jerome, the captain and eight policemen accompanied the SPC team to 43 Mercer Street where they had to knock down the locked door. Inside, they found forty men

engaged in illegal gambling. Two men who were identified as the proprietors of the establishment were arrested.

The next morning Captain Albertson was summoned to police headquarters where he had to explain to Murphy and Devery why he had failed to discover the gambling operation on Mercer Street before the SPC raid. Murphy departed police headquarters without addressing the issue with reporters. [38]

By reason of his frail health, caused by insufficient nourishment, the leader of the police department had the rooms in his home maintained at an extraordinarily high temperature. At police headquarters he had his office so warm that Devery soon began to swelter when he went in to talk over some subject with his nominal superior. One day the big deputy and the commissioner were in session together for an especially long time. It was just after the raid at 43 Mercer Street and all sorts of rumors were afloat through the corridors. The newspaper men eagerly awaited the end of the conference and when at last the door opened and Devery appeared on the threshold he was besieged with questions. He did not answer, but continued to mop his expansive face, from every pore of which the perspiration was pouring. After he had caught a cool breeze from an open window, he said, with a simultaneous gesture toward Murphy. "I was just telling the colonel that if he could keep the town as warm as he wants it himself, we wouldn't need the police. The crooks and bums would simply kill themselves. They would be more comfortable in the hereafter."

Justice Jerome would continue to be a thorn in Murphy's side for the duration of his tenure as police commissioner.

From 1894 to 1895, William Travers Jerome worked for the Lexow Committee. In 1894, he managed the successful campaign of William L. Strong for mayor of New York City. In 1895, the Court of Special Sessions was re-organized, legislating out of office the six incumbent justices. On July 1, 1895, Jerome took office as one of the first five new justices of the re-organized court.

A couple of days after the raid at Mercer Street Jerome made a demand to the Police Department Property Clerk that he bring all gambling paraphernalia that had been seized by the police in the raid to the criminal court in order that it could be burned. This order presented a problem because both the police and the gamblers expected that the gambling equipment would eventually make its way back to the gamblers. When the gambling paraphernalia never materialized at the courthouse, Jerome telephoned Property Clerk Lalor and repeated his demand that the gambling equipment be sent over immediately. Instead of gambling devices, Lalor, himself appeared in the courtroom holding a letter from Colonel Kipp, the Chief Clerk of the Police Department.

"Well, have you brought those gambling tools?" the judge snapped.

"No, I have not," replied Lalor.

"Why not?" demanded the judge.

In response, Lalor handed the letter to the judge, which read as follows: *I am directed by Police Commissioner Murphy to state that he is informed by the property clerk that an order was received by him over the telephone for delivery to you of all the roulette wheels seized in recent raids. The commissioner desires me to call to your attention that the property clerk is a bonded officer and is personally responsible for these implements now in his custody under the provisions of the statute and that he cannot deliver such material upon an order by telephone. If the articles are required for evidence, they will be produced by him upon a proper order. If they are to be destroyed the Commissioner desires me to call your attention to the provisions of the statutes that such destruction can only be made after conviction (section 245 of the penal code).*

Justice Jerome's face turned red as he read the letter. He growled that section 245 referred to the right to enter a gambling house and seize gambling tools and that those implements must be brought in front of the arraigning judge. He glared at Lalor and said, "You must have those gambling implements here by two o'clock this afternoon or I will have a warrant issued for your arrest.

Lalor mumbled under his breath as he departed the courtroom, but at two o'clock the courtroom was filled with gambling devices.

Despite the compliance with his order, Justice Jerome was still upset by the original stand taken by the police. "The police seem to be very anxious about this thing," he said. "I don't know why they are standing back of these people and making such a row about it."

"Well," Lalor sighed, "all I wanted to do was protect myself."

"I understand your position perfectly," replied Jerome, "but I am intimately acquainted with the administration of criminal law and have been for the last twelve years, but in that time, I never knew the police department to be so solicitous about letting gambling implements get out of their hands. I think it is a piece of impertinence on the part of the commissioner to attempt to instruct me in the premises, and I won't have it."

When made aware of Justice Jerome's remarks about him, Murphy said he would not reply to the judge's ill-chosen language. Language was the least of Murphy' problems, as he would soon discover that his problems with Jerome and other anti-corruption activists were just beginning. [39]

Chapter 4: Contradictions

In his effort to attempt to keep the mayor, his Tammany benefactors, and the people of the city happy, Murphy's tenure as police commissioner was filled with a string of contradictions.

On February 22nd Murphy was quoted in the newspapers as saying "I am going to be boss, as they say, because I am wholly responsible. I am going to enforce the law without fear or favor."

Two days later Murphy was quoted in the New York Times as saying, "I said yesterday that I would manage the police department as I did the health department, and that I wanted to be judged according to my acts and merits. That seems to me to cover the ground. I also said, by the way, that I would be supreme. Don't forget that."

Later that same day he made an address to the police captains, inspectors, and deputy chiefs, in which he repeated his declarations that he would be the actual head of the police department. But on February 25th Murphy published the following order to the police department:

"In pursuance of the authority invested in me by Chapter 33 of the Laws of 1901, I hereby delegate to first deputy commissioner of police the performance of all the duties which the chief of police performed prior to the passage of Chapter 33 of the Laws of 1901, except the power of making appointments and transfers. In the absence or disability of the first deputy commissioner of police, then and then only such duties shall devolve upon the second deputy commissioner of police to such extent as may be determined by the commissioner of police."

On February 28th Murphy sat for the first time to try policemen charged with offenses. He exhibited severity in the few cases upon which he passed judgement. He then called upon Deputy Commissioner Devery to preside and pass judgement in the remaining cases. Murphy did not try any complaints against policemen after that day.

On March 3rd Murphy was quoted in the newspapers as denying vigorously reports that he had abdicated certain of his functions in favor of Devery, and that a second deputy, who should practically have entire control of the police force in Brooklyn, would be appointed at the direction of the Kings County Democracy. But on March 4th in the New York Times Colonel Murphy declared that the appointment of a second deputy commissioner was still in abeyance, and his emphatic statement a day earlier that he would not be dictated to in the matter, caused some confusion in Brooklyn Democratic circles because it had been positively and authoritatively stated in Brooklyn that, on the strength of an agreement made between Murphy and Brooklyn political leader Shevlin, that the Brooklyn organization was to be allowed to name a man as second deputy commissioner, who would be permitted to run the Brooklyn police department with a free hand. Mr. Shevlin offered the appointment to Mr. York and the latter, after first declining, finally accepted.

The Brooklyn machine was stunned when they learned of Murphy's denial that Brooklyn would select his second deputy commissioner. Brooklyn Democrats were still strongly of the belief that York had been selected for the job, and that he would be named Murphy's second deputy commissioner.

James Shevlin, representing the Brooklyn Democratic machine, put the matter to rest when he traveled to police headquarters with Bernard York. They met briefly with Murphy after which a press conference was immediately held in which Murphy appointed York as his second deputy commissioner.

The contradictions continued with Murphy's quote in the Evening Post: "I am a newcomer, and only want to say that the gambling houses and disorderly houses and all other places wherein the law is violated must go. That is settled, they will and must go. I have ordered all captains to prepare a report containing all the places in their precinct which the law is being violated or suspected of being violated, and I will get those lists Friday morning. All these places will have to close up. No matter who says otherwise, they must obey the law."

Murphy then declared to reporters that he had taken special measures to discover gambling houses in operation. He was quoted as saying, "I am going to purify the city so that it will be clean and wholesome. I believe that we can put New York on a basis where we can be proud of it. The police are working in harmony with the district attorney who has furnished a list of alleged unlawful places."

Several weeks later Murphy was quoted in the New York Times as saying that he intended to raid the poolrooms and gambling houses, and that within two weeks not one such place would be left in the city. "I will show the people of this city that I am entitled to their confidence."

Murphy then summoned all the captains to a conference at headquarters. After the conference he told the reporters that he had instructed the captains to see that all the poolrooms and gambling houses were kept closed, and he threatened to "Break" any captain who did not carry out these instructions.

The quotes were impressive, and it appeared as if the new sheriff in town was going to run all the gamblers out of the city. But this was New York City under the rule of Tammany Hall, so Murphy couldn't really shut down the illegal gambling industry that Tammany depended on to line its pockets. Several weeks after making his bold declarations Murphy spoke for the first time about the results of his investigation. "The results of the investigations by my body of detectives were very fine. They were good reports and very encouraging, and the work continues. I told them, through Captain Titus, to scour the city. They were given the places on Mr. Nixon's list, 600 or 700 poolrooms, gambling houses, and other places where the law was habitually violated. I only know in a general way that very few places on the list appeared to be open. This result is very different from what the public has been led to believe."

The next day Murphy was asked by reporters to elaborate on his investigation of gambling houses, and he referred them to Captain Titus, head of the detective bureau. Titus said not one poolroom or gambling house had been found in operation.

The results of Murphy's "determined" efforts turned out to be two or three small raids by the police and his conclusion was that there was no collusion between the police and gamblers nor failure on the part of the police captains because there was no gambling in New York.

Commissioner Murphy was extremely naïve if he believed his statement that gambling didn't exist in the city would be enough to put the issue to bed. The remainder of his administration was filled with vice allegations and scandals. It reached the point where even gamblers made complaints. Such was the case with Patrick J. Murphy.

On July 19th, Patrick Murphy made a complaint about a poolroom operating in Long Island City. Murphy was not a reformer or anti-vice activist. Murphy was a bookmaker who didn't like gambling organizations from outside of Long Island City moving in on his action. The New York Times on the 20th quoted Murphy: "I hated to do this thing," he said, regretfully, "but I was forced to do it. We must protect ourselves. I belong to an organization which resents the invasion of our territory. I am a Gleasonite (Patrick Gleason was a political powerhouse and the former mayor of Long Island City when it was an independent municipality). Here is his pin. He gave it to me on his deathbed. I have always tried to live up to his principles. He believed in home rule, and so do I. I believe too, in equal rights to everybody and a fair chance to all. I'm a horseman and have been such for nineteen years. I've lived around here for 32 years. When there's any horse business doing, I want to be in it. I don't believe in any percentage business being done in this town, and I won't stand for it. No combination of Chicago or Buffalo, or New York or any other place can come in here and run this town or dictate to us. I won't stand for it. There has got to be a fair show. I don't give a damn for any Croker, or

Farrell or Sullivan or Devery or Minton or Casssidy. Mike Minton can't run this show from Williamsburg, and if I want to do business, I don't want to run to him for permission. I went up to a certain police official's office today and said a friend of mine wanted to open up. 'No,' said he. 'Well' said I, we ain't gonna stand for foreigners coming in here and doing business when we can't. There has to be a fair show. 'There won't be but one place open' said he. That was the one raided. I had to do it. I guess I'm the only member of the Gleason Organization who ever squealed, but this had to be done. We must protect ourselves. Tammany Hall is the closest corporation that ever happened, as many outsiders have been made to know; but nobody is going to come here and shut off those who have been here all their lives, and I know how to stop it, and I will if I have to.

Nothing more was heard from Commissioner Murphy on the subject, but on October 3rd the Chamber of Commerce adopted the following resolution:

Whereas, there is a widespread and well-founded belief in this city that certain officials in the police department are addicted to corrupt practices, and are soliciting and receiving moneys, for the wicked protection of vice and crime, thus encouraging the lawless element of this city to the detriment of decent and honest government, and to the endangering of life and property; and

Whereas, the charter of greater New York has conferred upon the mayor the high duty and responsibility of removing the head of any department that is incompetent or guilty of violations of law; therefore, be it

Resolved, the president of this Chamber be and hereby is directed to urge the mayor to exercise the supreme power vested in him to the end that the reproach now universally resting upon the government and good name of this city may be speedily removed.

Although the resolution did not explicitly say it, it was clear it was calling for the mayor to remove Police Commissioner Murphy from office. Murphy did not appear to be bothered by the resolution and other similar criticisms. He appeared to believe that it wasn't evil conditions that hurt the city – it was talking about them.

On March 9th he was quoted in the New York Times: "The department is demoralized on account of the attacks that have been made on it. If the police department were only let alone, and left to work out its own salvation, something could be done with it."

While sitting to hear complaints against policemen on August 16th Devery weighed in on how allegations of corruption hurt the city. "The charges are a libel on the city. Why, people coming here to buy goods stay away on the advice of their wives."

When the Merchant's Association complained to Murphy that the proliferation of vice in the city was hurting business, Murphy continued with his theme that there was "nothing to see here" by responding with a letter stating that the loss of commercial interests was the consequence of statements made by the association in the press regarding the existence of vice – not the actual existence of vice.

The Merchant's Association vehemently disagreed. This was in a circular early in October to a large number of merchants:

"The people of America are people of clean lives, moral, law-abiding, and God-fearing men and women. They turn with loathing and disgust from a city where vice is flagrant and unchecked. They despise a community whose moral forces are too feeble to resist and control crime. They regard with scorn and contempt a body of citizens who sluggishly surrender the machinery of public order, decency and safety to officials who promote crime in order that they may share its proceeds.

The business interests of this city come in direct contact with this widespread sentiment. Repugnance and resentment is the frequent expression of visiting merchants. It is the work of the Merchant's Association to resist that which threatens harm to business and property. Therefore, it seeks to drive from their positions those police officials who are disgracing the city and endangering its property."

On august 31, 1901 Mr. Leroy Dresser, as president of the Merchant's Association, wrote a letter to Murphy which read in part:

"I desire to call your attention to the scandals which are being published daily in the press concerning the police department of this city, and more particularly as regards to the effect of these disclosures upon the commercial interests of our city. I would urge you to probe these matters to the bottom at once. We believe that the men comprising the rank and file of our police department are honest, fearless and ready to do their duty. We have heard that a great many police officers are being transferred and otherwise punished simply because they do their duty. The recent developments show that these reports are not groundless."

On September 2nd, Murphy replied.: *"I most respectfully acknowledge our communication of the 31st inst. as president of the merchant's association of New York and agree with every word you say regarding the losses to your commercial interests in our city in consequence to the statements made in the press. I want to say, Mr. Dresser, that I will go as far as any man living to better the interests of the police department, as well as better the interests of the commercial community, and the proof is that there are no murders in New York; there are no robberies in New York; the citizens do not complain of any more gangs or thugs or ruffians assembling in various quarters of the city. Any man that passes through the streets of our city, at no matter what hour of the day or night, is not interfered with or insulted if he attends to his own business and goes along quietly and in an orderly manner. If politics could be eliminated from the press accounts of the police department there would be no occasion for the scandals that now exist. I am ready to cooperate with your society in anything you many suggest that can be carried out under the rules and under the law."*

On September 3rd Dresser responded: *"These and other evils which have been shown to exist have a bad effect upon the subordinates. Honest men on the force, and I believe they are in the majority, feel this and feel also that the disclosures which have been made reflect upon every member of the force and produce a wrong impression in the minds of the public concerning the integrity of many of these men. For their sake, as well as for the benefit of the commercial interests of the city, I repeat, that these matters ought to be probed to the bottom at once, and those responsible for existing conditions ought to be removed from office without hesitation and without delay. Demoralization, once started, is hard to check. The lack of discipline caused by this condition is already apparent to anyone who takes the trouble to look about him. The citizens of New York view this situation with alarm. I note what you say concerning your willingness to cooperate with us and thank you for the spirit which prompts the suggestion. I must say to you, however, that I do not see how it is possible for us to cooperate with you in your official work. The police department is given a liberal appropriation with which to maintain order and suppress vice. You, the responsible head of this great department, should move of your own volition. From my point of view it would be improper for us to move in an investigation of this kind; but I also feel that we would not be doing our duty to the great commercial interest of this city if we did not call attention to these matters and insist that you act without delay. We are not in politics, but as citizens and taxpayers we desire to see an efficient police administration. It is plainly apparent that the present administration is not efficient. It seems to us that it ought to be made so, at once."*

On September 4th Murphy replied by saying he was cooperating with the district attorney in investigating the corruption charges against the police department and took no further action regarding the Merchant's Association's complaint.[40]

Chapter 5: A Visit from Carrie Nation

The attacks from the Merchants' Association and other reform bodies continued, and only increased in frequency. Nothing, however, seemed to annoy Murphy as much as the visit of Carrie Nation to his office on August 28, 1901.

Caroline Amelia Nation, often referred to as Carrie A. Nation, or Hatchet Granny, was a radical member of the temperance movement, which opposed alcohol before the advent of Prohibition.

The hatchet wielding temperance terror used unorthodox, non-peaceful forms of protest that made her a national celebrity. Claiming to take directives directly from God, Nation battle axed her way through small Midwestern towns, protesting the sale of liquor with violent force, chopping at bar tops, bottles, and furniture with her signature hatchet, accompanied by a righteous choir of church ladies belting out hymns while dodging splinters.

Nation was regularly arrested and fined, but under the cover of doing God's duty — and riding a swell of anti-liquor sentiment — she managed to continue her vicious tirade across the country, becoming the temperance movement's most colorful star. She even sold miniature replicas of her well-known weapon to fund her cross-country adventures.

Nation's reputation had obviously preceded her when she arrived in New York on August 28, 1901. Law enforcement and nervous saloon owners braced for the worst. After freshening up in a suite of rooms arranged for her at the Victoria Hotel on 27th Street and Broadway, Mrs. Nation headed down to police headquarters on Mulberry Street to address the general drunkenness conditions of the city directly with Police Commissioner Murphy.

Their exchange was not pleasant. Nation demanded to know why the city kept saloons open on Sunday. Murphy replied that it was legal to do so. She bitterly lectured back with a Bible verse to which Murphy replied, "Don't quote scripture at me, Madame. Go back to Kansas and get that off on your husband."

"Are you angry because I want these rum hell holes closed?" said the hatcheteer, as she took a seat beside Murphy. Then, obtaining no answer, she added, "My father, are you angry?"

"What do you mean, madam?" replied Murphy, somewhat surprised. "I am not your father."

"I know it, but you look it. I am 35, and I'll wager you are 85, if a day. But there is no shame in being old, father."

Murphy wheeled around, so as to turn his back on the crusader.

"I've come to ask you to give an account of your stewardship," persisted the Kansas agitator. "Don't you think New York is an awfully bad place? Don't you think hatcheting would do it good?"

"If you violate the laws, I'll have you locked up," was Murphy's sharp reply.

After a few more volatile exchanges, Nation was forcefully removed from police headquarters, a result she had intended since her press agent was waiting outside to call out to a throng of curious onlookers that his client had been unceremoniously booted from police headquarters. Nation next decided to harangue the mayor and prepared to visit City Hall. When a message was sent that the mayor didn't care to meet with the fiery reformer, Nation decided to do what came most naturally – she headed for a bar, hatchet in hand.

The unfortunate establishment in her crosshairs was that owned by famed boxer John L. Sullivan, himself a celebrity of some flamboyance. Having spent the 1880s as one of America's most legendary bare-knuckle fighters, he was famously brought down (in a gloved match) by 'Gentleman' Jim Corbett in 1892. Like many boxing stars before him, Sullivan ended up in New York as a saloon owner, at 1177 Broadway, between 27th and 28th streets, very close to the hotel hosting Carrie Nation.

In a bit of braggadocio, Sullivan had proclaimed to the press that if Nation ever bothered to stop by, he would "thrust her into a sewer hole." Nation accepted the invitation, arriving by carriage and demanding Sullivan meet her out front. The famed boxer, however, refused to come outside, the New York Times even mentioning, "A shutter in one of the blinds in the room usually occupied by Mr. Sullivan was seen to move. The mighty athlete was certainly fearful of his property being chopped to ribbons. This wasn't some Bowery dive bar, after all. But while the authorities were certainly no friends of Nation, she was a very popular symbol among New York's temperance supporters. Arresting such a known figure would have actually played into Nation's intentions.

The great "John L." thought it best to wait out the storm. By the afternoon, Nation has left town via Grand Central, off to more wily stunts in the Midwest. John L. Sullivan, drinkers and cops alike raised a toast in relief. [41]

Chapter 6: O'Neill and Whitney

As Commissioner Murphy unsuccessfully attempted to keep the police department on a course free of controversy, two men – a patrolman and a private detective, caused Murphy to steer his police ship directly into the eye of the storm.

Edward O'Neill had served ten years in the regular army achieving the rank of first sergeant and had been a cop for twelve years. Whether or not he was a good cop or just a policeman who wanted to flaunt his authority was unknown, but what was apparent was that O'Neill was fed up with the impact corruption was having on his personal life.

O'Neill lived with his family in the Bronx in close proximity to the Tremont Avenue station house. During a span of four months O'Neill had been transferred six times because he refused to pay a $45 fee to remain at Tremont Avenue. It wasn't until he finally paid the fee that he was returned to Tremont Avenue.

In today's NYPD transfers to a precinct far from home are an annoyance, but nothing more. Public transportation and cars make every precinct in the city reachable within a reasonable period of time. In 1901, a transfer to a precinct far from home was devastating. Cops were already working long hours and adding hours of travel time could make the job almost impossible.

In 1901 New York City had many active Blue Laws requiring most businesses to be closed on Sundays, or at least a portion of the day. Elias Hollander was a Hebrew Dealer in tinware &crockery at 3806 Third Avenue, in the Bronx. On Sunday, August 11th at 9:30 A.M. he was exchanging some goods for a woman customer when Patrolman O'Neill came to the door and told him he was violating the law by selling goods on Sunday. Hollander said his store and all the other stores were allowed to be open until 10 A.M. Hollander told his son to close the door and went back attending to his customer. According to

Hollander, O'Neill entered and roughly arrested him, and would not let him go into the back room to get his coat, finally pulling his revolver out.

Hollander made a formal complaint against O'Neill, creating an exciting scene in the trial room at 300 Mulberry Street when First Deputy Commissioner Devery presided over O'Neill's department trial.

O'Neill was charged with breaking into a store on Sunday morning, arresting the owner for violating the Sunday Law, dragging him to the station house after clubbing him and threatening to shoot him, and also for arresting the man's son, who tried to protect his father. It was alleged that the storekeeper, in the presence of the policeman, had sold to a woman six plates. After a dozen witnesses had proved the case against O'Neill, the policeman said he drew his pistol in self-defense.

"They ought to have thrown you out the window," interrupted Devery. "What good would it have done that woman if she had bought meat or vegetables or other stores and had no plates to put them on."

"I obeyed orders from the station house," said O'Neill, "and I had to protect my life."

"We have had enough of that," thundered Devery. "You ought to join Carrie Nation and the tin soldiers she had come here to reinforce her. It is the rottenest piece of business on the part of the people who are inciting to riot. You ought to constitute yourself a fifth party and get an axe, as she and the rest of them are doing. And then go around and wreck stores. It is a bloody outrage," he repeated. "Just think of it. One raving maniac – a woman- comes to town, and other lunatics are crazy to follow in her footsteps. It is a bloody outrage the way certain people in this town are going on at the present time, and it is about time it was stopped. They are like a lot of madmen let loose from a lunatic asylum, trying to terrorize a city with four million of population. Those who are doing this have a lot to answer for, and I cannot, to save my life, understand why people tolerate it."

"I did my duty!" cried O'Neill.

"You did not," snapped Devery, "and because you did not, I'll fine you thirty days."

"You will not!" screamed O'Neill. "I'll not stand for it. I'll go higher up."

"You'll take it," cried Devery

"I won't!" shouted O'Neill. "If I had stood for another shakedown and given up when asked to, I suppose I would have been alright."

"What's that?" cried Devery.

O'Neill was a slender rawboned old Irish policeman who was ready to burst at Devery as he repeated his previous statement as he headed for the door. "I suppose if I'd stand a shakedown you'd stand for it. I've been transferred six times in four months because I won't stand a shaking down. I paid $45 –"

Devery heard the statement as O'Neill was leaving. "Come back here. What did you say?"

O'Neill walked right up to Devery and stared him in the eyes. "I said that I have been transferred six times in the last four months, and I wouldn't stand for a shakedown." He then turned and walked toward the door.

Devery was in a rage such as he had never shown in the trial room before. He got partly up from his seat, clutching at the desk in front of him. He was speechless for a moment, and then yelled at the top of his lungs, "I'll make a complaint of insubordination against you and I'll break you."

"Go ahead and do it," O'Neill shouted back.

"You're a loafer. Get out of here." Devery shouted as O'Neill left the room. "And you will be examined as to your mental condition also."

As he stood by the door O'Neill openly defied Devery by shaking his fist in his face and again stating he would not stand for the thirty days fine but would take it higher up.

"I'll not have you or any other man in this department stand for these blue laws that permit men's homes to be broken into by tin soldiers" Devery shouted.

O'Neill was pushed into the corridor. Devery, who was white with rage, then called the next case.

As O'Neill went downstairs, he said, "The reason I'm being persecuted is because I refused to give up $45 not to be transferred."

He then proceeded to the District Attorney's office where he met ADA Gans, to whom he said, "I've been persecuted with consistent regularity since last April, when I made an excise arrest in the Twenty-Seventh Precinct. Since then, I have been transferred six times and complaints have been made against me for no reason whatsoever."

O'Neill then enumerated several cases for which he said he had been fined from five to ten days each. O'Neill said he was attacked by Hollander, his wife and son, and was simply defending himself.

O'Neill spent the remainder of the afternoon talking with the ADA and Justice Jerome. When Murphy was told of O'Neill's allegation of having to pay to avoid a transfer he said, "That's the first that I have ever heard such information."

The next day, Murphy transferred O'Neill back to his home precinct in Tremont. In questioning O'Neill about having to pay to avoid being transferred, Murphy could not get O'Neill to reveal who had solicited the money. O'Neill said the revelation would be pointless because it would be his word against the other person's word. Murphy did, however, get O'Neill to confirm that it was not Devery who asked him for money. He asked the question about Devery in the presence of reporters. Murphy assured O'Neill he would not be injured again and would remain at the Tremont station. [42]

Despite Murphy's assurances to O'Neill, Devery moved forward with his charges of insubordination and a trial was scheduled for O'Neill. When asked about why the charges were proceeding, Murphy said, "O'Neill made certain charges against the police department. Either the department or certain men in it are guilty of what he alleges or there is no foundation to his charges. This is the time to find out the truth and I propose to find it. That is the reason we are putting this man on trial. We want to get to the bottom of this thing and the only way to do it is to get at the facts through a trial."

Murphy said that neither he nor Devery would act at the trial, and that Deputy Commissioner York would preside.

When O'Neill's trial got underway, one of the witnesses who testified on behalf of O'Neill was Patrolman John Marrinan. It may have been coincidence, but a week after the trial, while Deputy Commissioner York weighed his decision, Marrinan found himself back in the trial room, facing the wrath of the man he had testified against – Big Bill Devery.

Marrinan had been charged by Inspector Cross with appearing for inspection at the Eldridge Street station house on September 9th in trousers that were "filthy and unfit."

Marrinan said to a reporter, "I'm not a squealer, and I don't want to say anything. My clothes was dirty but I had been having a time with a prisoner the night before and that accounts for it."

Once the hearing began, Devery asked, "What's the charge against this man?"

"His clothes were dirty," responded Inspector Cross, who had a reputation for being one of the nattiest dressers in the department. "His trousers are absolutely sickening."

Devery was angry and also appeared to be gloating. "What have you to say to this, Marrinan?" Devery asked.

Marrinan appeared pale and trembling. "I had a woman prisoner the night before, and she dirtied them."

"Did she put your clothes on?" sneered Devery.

"No, sir, but she was very unclean."

"Unclean," shouted Devery. "No matter how filthy she was she was cleaner than you – you-" Devery stopped in mid-sentence, choked with rage.

Marrinan's face turned red and he appeared to be angered by the remark, but he remained composed and replied timidly, "I don't think so, sir."

Devery turned to Inspector Cross. "What excuse did he make to you?"

Marrinan attempted to interrupt before the Inspector could respond. "Now – now"

"Now, now," bellowed Devery, "just spit it out. You're a bum. Clear out of here and keep clear of me."

"So –" Marrinan attempted to speak but was again cut off by the deputy commissioner.

"I'll fine you fifteen days pay. Now go, you loafer – you dirty bum, you."

Marrinan left the room in a daze.

Devery took a deep breath and smiled. "Next case," he called out.

Reporters informed Murphy that during the trial Devery had referred to Marrinan as a loafer and a dirty bum.

"Do you stand for such language as that?" the commissioner was asked.

"He didn't say that, did he?" Murphy replied.

"Yes, those remarks were made," a reporter confirmed.

"Well, he couldn't have made those remarks as an official. He was just talking in his private capacity. They certainly didn't go on the record."

Once again, Murphy tried to thread the needle in responding to his deputy commissioner's actions.[43]

Devery's less than civil nature was also on full display in the case of Patrolman William Monahan. 65-year-old Monahan had been a patrolman for 41-years, spending most of those years assigned near the Casino in Central Park. Monahan and his father, who was a landscape gardener, helped to lay out Central Park, and almost everyone who had ever gone to the Casino knew Patrolman Monahan. The gray-haired officer with his long and honorable service to the department was universally respected by all.

Unfortunately, Monahan made the mistake of enforcing a park ordinance by making a man at the Casino put his dog back in his carriage. The man was a known gambler named Lamar, who happened to be a good friend of Deputy Commissioner Devery. Lamar made a complaint to Big Bill, and Monahan was quickly charged and brought before Devery, who promptly transferred Monahan to a distant precinct.

When Devery was asked about his treatment of Monahan, he said, "He's an old dub and an old dope. He ought to get out of the business long ago. I did right to transfer him. He should have resigned years ago. There's lots of citizens complained of him. He's an old dope, I say, and ought to resign."

A reporter pointed out that Monahan seemed to be doing his duty by making the man put his dog in the carriage.

"I won't have a policeman interfere with the rights of citizens," said Devery. "If a man comes up for the Casino and has the price to pay for his refreshment, I won't have him interfered with. That policeman overreached himself in this matter. I won't have policemen overreachin themselves like this."

A reporter asked if Monahan was given the opportunity to speak in his own defense.

"Now, see here," said Devery, "I tell you this man was an old dub. He's over 60-years old and ought to be out of this business. There's a lot of these old dopes who ought to get out of the way and make room for young blood. They ought to retire and spend some of their money going around the world seeing the sights. That's all there is to this case."

Monahan said that he could not stand a transfer and that if he had to leave his present assignment, he would be forced to quit. Therefore, he submitted his application for retirement which Commissioner Murphy quickly approved. As was frequently the case, Murphy claimed ignorance of the details of Monahan's dealings with Mr. Lamar in Central Park, claiming that all he knew was what he read in the newspaper. The reporters, however, were not going to let Murphy off the hook so easily, and one asked the commissioner if he agreed with Devery's characterization of Monahan and other older officers as "old dopes."

"Now, I'm not going to comment on that," said Murphy, "but I don't mind saying that I do not believe in eliminating the old men on the force."

Monahan continued to exhibit class when he was asked about his retirement. "I will not talk against my superiors no matter what they say of me. I went on the force forty years ago with a good character and I want to leave it the same way." [44]

It may have seemed that Devery was a harsh judge when he presided over police trials, but this was not always the case. Indicative of his idea of what the moral qualities of a policeman ought to be, Devery once refused to dismiss from the force a policeman who had been sentenced to state prison for seducing a fifteen-year-old girl with whom he had been living in adultery, while refusing to support his wife, who had been compelled to put their children in a charitable institution. In fact, his adjudication in this case prompted the only time Commissioner Murphy overruled Devery's decision. [45]

In February 1892 Patrolman McManus, though married, was found to be living with a fifteen-year-old girl named Mary Jennings. The girl was rescued by the Gerry Society and McManus was tried before Police Commissioner Sheehan for conduct unbecoming an officer. The decision in the case was reserved.

On March 5, 1892, McManus was held for trial in General Sessions on the charge of rape. After a number of arraignments and adjournments, Judge Martine dismissed the indictment on a technicality. Later, the matter of McManus's family was investigated and it was found that he had a wife and four children, all of whom were destitute. A warrant was issued for the arrest of McManus, but he had disappeared. It was stated that he had been dismissed from the police force for neglect of duty and intoxication. The children were committed to semi-public institutions.

In 1898 McManus was summoned to court by his wife for non-support. He promised the court that he would pay her $6 a week, and he was released, but he did not keep his promise and on Jan 21, 1901, he was arraigned in the Fourth District City Magistrate Court. He admitted on that occasion that he was living with a Mrs. Daly at 267 Tenth Avenue. On January 24th, before Justice Jacobs, McKeon and Jerome, in the Court of Special Sessions, McManus was sentenced to three months in the penitentiary for not paying support for his children.

Through these years McManus served 3-months and 6-months in the penitentiary, but somehow managed to remain on the police force. When his case was the subject of a departmental rial, Deputy Commissioner Devery dismissed the case, and McManus remained on the police force.

Devery was asked why he would dismiss the case against a man with the record outlined by Justice Jerome during the criminal case.

"I have not seen it," Devery said.

A reporter then outlined McManus's record and asked if Devery knew the record was that bad when he dismissed the case.

"I dismissed it because his captain told me he was a good man," said the deputy commissioner. "That's all there is to it."

"Do you think a man with a record like that is fit to be on the force?" a reporter asked.

"No man is guilty till it's proved. Oh, I know he was up for three months – and again for six months, but Captain Cooney assured me that he was a good officer. Why, during a riot McManus put out eighteen or twenty men all by himself. The law says you can't dismiss a man because he has been convicted of a misdemeanor. As I said before, the captain said he was alright, and that ended it."

The reporters kept pressing for any reason why McManus would be kept on the force. The visibly annoyed Devery huffed, "There are reasons unknown to me and unknown to you," before walking away.[46]

On September 24th, Deputy Commissioner York found O'Neill guilty of conduct unbecoming an officer. York based his decision on the fact that when O'Neill made the statement that he would not stand for another shakedown, he was inferring that if he paid money, Devery would drop the charges against him. O'Neill admitted that was the meaning of his statement, and York said that it was a charge of dishonesty made against a superior officer that O'Neill later admitted was false. Later in the day Murphy dismissed O'Neill from the force but declined to make any comment on the case.[47]

If Murphy thought that dismissing O'Neill from the force would silence the issue forever, he was badly mistaken. Seth Low was running for mayor on a fusion ticket against Tammany Hall, and O'Neill became active in the Low campaign. On October 22nd he gave a speech to a crowd on police corruption just two doors down from Murphy's Broome Street home.[48]

O'Neill made numerous speeches for the fusion ticket and they paid him a salary equal to his police pay. After the election they found him work with a comparable salary, and he hoped that on January 1st, 1902, when the new mayor took office, he would be reinstated.[49]

Devery found himself in hot water over the O'Neill case when the District Attorney's office brought criminal charges against him for oppression and extortion.

Oppression and extortion were described as follows in the penal code:

Oppression and extortion committed under color of official right. A public officer or a person pretending to be such, who unlawfully and maliciously, under pretense or color of official authority (1) arrests another or detains him against his will: (2) seizes or levies upon another's property: or, (3) dispossesses another of any lands or tenements: or (4) does any other act, whereby another is injured in his person, property, or right, commits oppression and is guilty of a misdemeanor.

Assistant District Attorney Osborne handled the case against Devery, and he said the acts of oppression by Devery consisted of his failure to give Policeman O'Neill a fair trial and fining him thirty days pay without allowing him to call all the witnesses he had in his behalf. Osborne further stated that with all the investigations and information regarding Devery, the District Attorney felt that the charges based on the O'Neill case had the best chance of gaining a conviction.[50]

Despite Devery's behavior toward O'Neill, including calling him a bum and a loafer, the case against him was dismissed. In dismissing the case, Justice Holbrook said, "In my judgement, no conviction for any neglect of duty, based upon this charge alone, would legally stand. While the conduct of the defendant, sitting as trial judge, was indecorous and offensive, yet I know of no precedent where a person acting in a judicial capacity has been punished criminally or civilly, for language used in condemning a party to the action. Entertaining the views I do, the complaint against William S. Devery is dismissed and the defendant is discharged." Once again, Big Bill had skated. [51]

The situation took a turn for the worse for O'Neill when the new administration took office, but new Police Commissioner Partridge said he would not reinstate O'Neill because he was against reinstating officers who had been dismissed. O'Neill still had supporters, however, and a bill was introduced in the Legislature in Albany calling for O'Neill's reinstatement. The bill passed and finally reached Mayor Low, who signed O'Neill's reinstatement on May 19, 1903.[52]

On 5/21/01, While Commissioner Murphy was still trying to convince the city that no illegal gambling houses were open, Justice Jerome and the committee of fifteen descended upon a poolroom in a saloon on Front Street. Two men were arrested, and various gambling equipment was confiscated.

Justice Jerome said, "This affair is simply one of the series which we intend will rid the city of poolrooms. I am receiving letters daily from poor people who have lost their money through poolrooms and gambling houses." [53]

As Commissioner Murphy continued to question the existence of open pool rooms and gambling houses in the city, Justice Jerome joined with Frank Moss and the SPC to increase the frequency of the pool room raids.

Frank Moss was an American lawyer, reformer and author. He was involved in many of the reform movements in New York City shortly before the start of the 20th century up until his death. He became involved in "vice crusades" and other reform movements while studying to pass the bar. Early in his legal career, he held important positions such as president of the Society for the Prevention of Crime

Moss first came to prominence during the Lexow hearings, as an associate council where he established himself as an aggressive prosecutor and investigator. While cross-examining Richard Croker, Moss was able to provoke him into stating the now famous statement admitting his corruption: "I am working for my pocket all the time, just like you, Mr. Moss."

In 1897, he succeeded Theodore Roosevelt as president of the Board of Police Commissioners. In 1901, during Seth Low and Justice William Jerome's campaign against the city's red-light districts, Moss famously addressed the court in a speech blaming Croker for the existence of white slavery and forced prostitution.

To counteract Murphy's denials, and to keep the pressure on the illegal gambling establishments, the SPC had to hire more private investigators to conduct their operations. 34-year-old Edgar A. Whitney was a man on a mission when he joined the SPC. His mission, however, was not to rid the city of vice. Whitney's mission was to make money. He quickly discovered the quickest way to the most money was to use his inside knowledge to tip off the gamblers of impending SPC raids. This situation worked well, but not well enough to suit Whitney. The more tips he could provide to the gamblers the more money he could make. Therefore, he was going to have to find more Parkhurst agents looking to make good money.

Whitney's initial intuition was good when he partnered with a man named Bergdorf, but even their combined efforts could not garner enough information to suit Whitney. He set his sights on bringing another agent into the fold. After an SPC meeting Whitney and Bergdorf approached an agent named Charles Dillon and told him of the large amount of money available to him in their scheme to tip off the gambling houses of SPC raids. Whitney offered to pay Dillon $250 a month for notification of impending raids. Dillon said that when he received the information the raids would be occurring very soon thereafter, and he didn't understand how the tips could be communicated quick enough to be of value. Whitney said notification to the precincts could be made through the police headquarters operators. Dillon asked how it was possible to make such communications over the police wires, and Whitney smiled and said that Devery had ordered the operators to make any connections requested by Whitney.

Dillon agreed to help, and the trio of conspirators shook hands. Whitney and Bergdorf headed for a local saloon, but Dillon declined an offer to join them, saying he had an important matter to attend to. That important matter turned out to be informing Frank Moss immediately of the "tipping" scheme he had just been made aware of.[54]

The next day Dillon made an appointment to Meet Whitney at the SPC office at 105 East 22nd Street. The purpose of the meeting was supposed to be to look over some new men for the agency, but Whitney was about to fall into a carefully laid trap set by Frank Moss. As soon as he entered the office, Moss declared Whitney to be under arrest on a warrant issued by Justice Jerome. A shocked Whitney ran to the corner of the room and threw a bundle of papers out the window which were picked up by a policeman who had been posted outside for such a purpose. When Moss received the papers, they turned out to be duplicate copies of the poolroom locations Whitney had provided to Dillon at the time of their arrangement.

Ten minutes after Whitney fell into Moss's trap, a tall, slim man entered a phonebooth on a street not far from the SPC office and rang up police headquarters.

"Who are you?" asked the police operator at headquarters.

"Bergdorf – Whitney's partner."

There was silence on the line until Captain Vredreburg at the Oak Street station house repeated the police operator's question. "Who is this?"

"This is Bergdorf – Whitney's partner."

"What Whitney?" the captain asked.

"Edgar A. Whitney – the Parkhurst Society is raising hell. They have a number of warrants for places in your precinct. They will have to be closed. There is one for 33 Park Row."

"32 Park Row?"

"No, 33 Park Row."

"Alright."

Inside 33 Park Row a short, chubby bald man was busy near the cashier planning his next bet. The cashier cried out, "Fourth race at

Saratoga." He then looked toward the bald man. "What do you say?" Several men rushed to the cashier's window before the bald man, but before any bets were taken, the cashier screamed, "Police outside!"

Forty to fifty men joined the bald man in pouring out of 33 Park Row. Some of the establishment workers carried with them the contents and gambling paraphernalia of the room.

The fleeing men scattered in all directions. The chubby bald man trotted north for three blocks before stopping to catch his breath. Agent McClintock, of the SPC, approached the breathless man. Well?" he asked.

The bald man, also an agent of the SPC, took a couple of deep breaths before speaking. "They received a tip," he nodded.

At another location, an informant identified a patrolman named Glennon as the person who provided the tip of the imminent raid.

In order to make a final test of the "tipping" system, Moss was able to have alarms sent to thirty or forty poolrooms over the headquarters wires. Within fifteen minutes thereafter Parkhurst agents stationed in front of the poolrooms saw a hasty exit of the patrons and managers carrying the money and paraphernalia of the betting establishments to places of safety. Bergdorf was subsequently arrested and both he and Whitney were brought before Justice Jerome to be arraigned.[55]

Whitney and Bergdorf were charged with conspiracy and aiding and abetting gamblers and held in $3,000 bail. When Justice Jerome adjourned court for the lunch break Bergdorf remained composed, but Whitney was visibly shaken at the prospect of being thrown into a cell in the Tombs jail. Justice Jerome had only walked down Centre Street as far as Chambers Street when a breathless messenger caught up with him. Whitney wanted to make a confession. Jerome hastily returned to his courtroom and had Whitney brought before him. Mr. Friend, Whitney's attorney, begged him not to make a statement, but Whitney did not want to return to the cell in the tombs. In return for his release, he made a full confession.

Whitney talked about the arrangements he had with the proprietors of thirty or more poolrooms and the representatives of the police department in the "tipping" of the poolrooms respecting impending raids by the Parkhurst Society. Whitney's disclosures implicated patrolman Edward G. Glennon, who was a close friend of Deputy Commissioner Devery. Devery was mentioned several times in Whitney's revelations to Justice Jerome, but his testimony regarding Devery was not sufficiently strong or direct to implicate him in a conspiracy.[56]

When Moss and Jerome released their new information to the newspapers, they were hoping to receive some response from the police department. At police headquarters there was every indication that the revelations made regarding police protection of gamblers had a decided effect, as nerves were on edge throughout the building.

Commissioner Murphy arrived from his summer home in Far Rockaway at 9 o'clock but Deputy Commissioner Devery was not seen all day, and Murphy said he was still in Saratoga on vacation.

Murphy was immediately questioned about Mr. Moss's disclosures, and he said he only knew what he read in the newspapers. The commissioner said he was launching an investigation but denied that any of his captains were involved in tipping off gamblers, and that he was looking into the conduct of the telephone operator who had been on duty on the day of the alleged tips to the poolrooms.

When asked if he would be investigating Devery's conduct also, Murphy responded, "You know, newspaper reporters, when they don't write shorthand will make some mistakes. I used to be a compositor myself and know that mistakes can easily be made, and sentences made to read differently than they should. I think that you will find in a few days that these charges will be modified. It seems to me rather peculiar that Deputy Commissioner Devery could have given the purported order. It is also queer that this order could have been sent out and over the telephone without all the men downstairs knowing about it. You know what human nature is."

Devery returned from Saratoga a few days later and did not seem at all phased by the turmoil at police headquarters. He went right to work presiding over police trials and even made some remarks during a trial that were dripping with sarcasm regarding the "tipping scandal."

Patrolman John Hessian, of the tenderloin precinct, was accused by Roundsman Sennett of being off post and inattentive to his duties while he engaged in conversation with a woman for seventeen minutes.

"Why didn't you see the roundsman?" Devery asked the patrolman, "are you near sighted?"

"No, sir, my back was turned to him," Hessian replied.

"Well," Devery continued, "if you was standing with your back to the roundsman, the lady must have been facing him. Didn't she tip you off?"

"No, sir."

"Well, there's a good deal of 'tippin' going on nowadays. I wouldn't stand talking fifteen minutes with a young lady who wouldn't 'tip' me off when the roundsman came up. And when you're caught with the goods on you and can't get away with it you want to stand up with nerve and take your medicine. You don't know nothing then. No matter under what circumstances, a man doesn't want to know nothing when he's caught with the goods on him. Don't stand up here and try to throw your roundsman when he's got you right. You tell that young lady when you're talking to her next time that when you've got your back to the roundsman she must look the other way. Always get 'tipped' off. Now, I'll fine you ten days pay for not getting 'tipped' off." [58]

Chapter 7: Murphy's Obsession

Colonel Murphy spent much of his time as police commissioner denying the existence of most crime and vice in New York City. For reasons that were never clear, there was one law Murphy vigorously enforced, but only against one man.

In 2021, nearly a century after it was passed, a law that banned residents of New York State from selling a shave or a haircut on Sundays was finally repealed. New York Governor Andrew Cuomo officially took the law off the books, calling it an archaic and meaningless piece of legislation that makes little to no sense in the 21st century. While he noted that the law was rarely enforced anymore, he said that he was more than happy to sign this repeal into law and allow these businesses to determine what days they choose to operate.

The now-defunct edict, Section 16 of the General Business section of the Consolidated Laws of New York, was one of many so-called "blue laws," meaning that it prohibited a certain activity or activities on Sunday for religious purposes. Historically, for example, the sale of alcohol was so regulated. As recently as 2016, Cuomo repealed a blue law that banned bars and restaurants from serving alcoholic beverages before noon on Sundays.

In 1907, Assemblyman Alfred E. Smith of Manhattan, seeking to legalize Sunday baseball, argued that it was more ennobling for young men to watch a game at an open-air ballpark than to "be driven to places where they play 'Waltz Me Around Again, Willie.'"

By 1919, baseball was permitted by local option. In 1937, bowling was allowed. In 1949, the Legislature decriminalized football, basketball and soccer after 2 p.m. In 1952, bans on stock car racing, circuses, hunting and golf were lifted. In 1973, Sunday horse racing was legalized.

Back in 1901 most of these Sunday blue laws were in effect in New York City, including a ban against establishments serving alcohol and allowing dancing on Sunday.

Little by little these blue laws were successfully challenged in court, and in 1901 Justice Andrews threw out the New York City ban on Sunday dancing. That court decision didn't stop Commissioner Murphy, however, from performing what he considered to be his public duty.

Louis Waldron operated a dancehall on the West Side of Manhattan at 110th Street, in an area known as "Little Coney Island." On a Sunday near the end of May 25-uniformed police officers under the command of Inspector Grant and Captain Kemp, marched into the dancehall and sat at the tables lining the dancefloor. The cops proceeded to smoke and read newspapers at the tables while Inspector Grant announced that anyone observed dancing would be arrested.

Mr. Steinhardt, Waldron's attorney, attempted to explain to Inspector Grant that a court decision had made dancing a legal Sunday activity, and that it was appropriate for the police to inspect the dancehall for illegal activity, but not appropriate for the police to remain inside smoking and reading the newspaper waiting for an illegal activity to occur. Inspector Grant said his contingent of policemen would not leave, prompting the attorney to recommend that Waldron close and lock the dancehall. With the police still unwilling to leave, Waldron began the process of physically removing the police from the site, but three people were quickly arrested.

The next day Commissioner Murphy was present at the West Side Police Court as Magistrate Zeller adjudicated the case. Under Murphy's administration the dancehall had been shut down with arrest almost every Sunday, as this present case marked the 17th incident. Zeller was frustrated with Murphy's action, and he let the police commissioner know it.

"You, Colonel Murphy," said the Magistrate, as he pointed to Louis Waldron, "had no right to cause this man's arrest seventeen times when a decision of Justice Andrews deemed him guiltless, and the magistrate discharged your prisoners. If the police department construes laws to suit itself and pays no attention to the courts, what are we coming to? What sort of state of civilization is that?"

"The case was faked up," responded Murphy. "When the Corporation Counsel, who is my legal advisor, shall show me such a decision and tell me that it is law, I will defer to it."

Louis Waldron testified that before this most recent arrest he had traveled with his attorney to see Commissioner Murphy and had shown him the decision rendered by Justice Andrews.

"I handed him the court decision," Waldron said, "and told him that dancing was legal on Sunday and that he was ruining my business." Waldron said the commissioner responded by saying, "Decision or no decision, I'll arrest everybody in your place."

Zeller turned his attention to the police lawyer. "Don't you know that Justice Andrews' decision is law?" demanded Zeller.

"It is law in a way," replied the lawyer. "That is to say it a decision of a judge that hasn't been overruled yet."

"Independent of this case," Zeller growled with considerable anger, "to hold that the decision that Sunday dancing is legal is the only law on the subject and the police department can't disregard it. You can't keep on this way, Commissioner Murphy. The courts make the laws, and the courts will keep discharging your prisoners."

"When the Corporation Counsel informs me, I will act accordingly," Murphy declared.

As all parties were leaving the building, Mr. Steinhardt got in the final word to the police attorney. "It's a pretty small business for the general of an army to declare after the guns have been fired that he didn't give the order for firing." [58]

Chapter 8: The Button

On June 11, 1901, the police wire flashed the following order to all the station houses in the city.

Ordered, That Paragraph C of Rule 31, relative to buttons, is amended to read as follows:

Buttons – Coat of arms of the City of New York, made to conform with the great Seal of the City of New York, now used and approved at the City Hall. This coat of arms is surrounded by a highly burnished, bright, flat ring. Between this and the burnished outer ring of the button are the words "New York City Police," surrounded by a five pointed star, all brought out in the highest artistic relief. The shell of these buttons is made of the best gilding metal, known as Prince's Metal Oreide. These shells are extra heavy, double plated by the fire gilding or amalgamating process with 24-carat fine gold, and they will not change color or become tarnished when exposed to the air. The backs are good brazing brass, known as French gilt, and burnished to preserve the cloth they come in contact with on the coats. The fastening of the buttons shall be a patented two pronged wire with spring attachment, and inside securing plate, as per sample in cloth room.

The above is transmitted for the information and guidance of the police force.

M.C. MURPHY

Commissioner and Chief of Police

During the months he had been police commissioner Murphy had been besieged with numerous problems and issues. Would he institute the three-platoon system in the department and how would he handle the growing number of vice committees, gambling crusaders, and similar groups besetting him? Through it all, partially due to his weakened physical condition, Murphy always maintained a calm composure. On June 12th, however, he bristled at the first question from a reporter.

"Will you comment about the order regarding the buttons, commissioner?"

"There isn't any such order," Murphy snapped.

When a reporter showed him the order, his face took on an angry scowl. "Buttons!" he exclaimed, "what do I know about buttons? Oh, bother, the button!"

"Must the policemen supply themselves with the new button as originally ordered by July 1st?" he was asked.

"I don't know," Murphy answered.

"Will –"

"I don't know anything about it," Murphy interrupted. "I'm not in their confidence."

"But the order –"

"I'm not in their confidence," he repeated, as he slid into the elevator and disappeared.

Why was Murphy so upset about questions regarding an order he published? Perhaps it had just occurred to him that with all the other problems he was facing, he had just created a new scandal all by himself – a scandal that would be known as the "Murphy Button."

Before consolidation New York City consisted mostly of Manhattan, but on January 1, 1898, the consolidation joined Manhattan to Brooklyn, Queens, Staten Island, and the Bronx, to form the Greater City of New York that we know today.

The consolidation brought the Brooklyn police and all the police from the independent towns and villages in Brooklyn and Queens into the New York City Police Department.

Consolidation brought the need for many changes in the police department ranging from the abolition and creation of titles to changes in uniforms and station houses. John McCullagh was the chief of police at the time of the consolidation, and before he was forced out to make room for Tammany's "Best Police Chief in History," Big Bill Devery, McCullagh made the necessary changes, including a specific change to the police uniform. With policemen from over eighteen different departments joining the NYPD, McCullagh realized he needed to standardize the uniform. One of these changes was the introduction of a new button for policemen to wear on their shirts and coats. These new uniform buttons became known as "Consolidation Buttons."

The old consolidation buttons were made of brass and bore the Great Seal of New York City with no words. The new "Murphy Buttons" were double-plated with 24-carat gold, and along with the Great Seal were the words "New York City Police" on the face of the button. The new button also had a new design where it fastened by a new patent design which made sewing unnecessary.

A logical person would question why there would be a need to change the uniform buttons in the first place. Murphy made the rather incredulous statement that police officers could not be identified as such and were being mistaken for streetcar conductors.

Immediately, the members of the force were irate, not only because they were forced to pay for the buttons themselves, but because of the comparatively exorbitant cost (15 cents per button) compared to the existing consolidation buttons (7 cents each).

One newspaper reported the details of the quantities needed. "Each man needs a blouse and a dress suit. The latter required thirteen large buttons and six small ones. The blouse, four large buttons. A winter suit, which will not be required for a few weeks, will require twenty-two large buttons and six small ones." The article estimated that approximately 500,000 buttons would be needed.

The question being asked in police circles around the city was who in the department had gone into the button business. Not only did there seem to be no real need for new buttons, but the unique new design of the new button would limit the options of where they could be purchased. A law passed in Albany in 1900 allowed policemen and firemen to buy any articles of their uniform wherever they pleased, so as to break up a promising cloth monopoly in connection with firemen's uniforms. But with the new patented fastening method of the new "Murphy Button," there would be only one choice as to where the buttons could be obtained. But the question was still where that one location would be. [59]

On June 13th, with Commissioner Murphy still refusing to discuss the new buttons, an ex-judge named A.J. Dittenhoefer came forward to state he was organizing a company to manufacture the new button in the interest of the inventor, Ethel Phelps. Murphy was forced to extend the July 1st date for all policemen to obtain the new buttons, and on July 2nd he signed a contract with Ethel Phelps to furnish the department with 5,000 gross of uniform buttons. [60]

It wasn't until October that the new buttons were finally ready for distribution, and the policemen were compelled to dig into their own pockets to furnish their three uniforms with the new buttons. It would cost every policemen in the city $1.97 more to furnish his uniform with the new buttons than with the old ones. Another factor that outraged the cops was that the old buttons would have to be thrown away. The new buttons rendered them useless despite the fact that they were only a few years old and still in good condition. There was additional grumbling from the police because the consensus was that the new buttons were not as well made as the old buttons.

The button came in two sizes, a large one for the front of the coat and a smaller one for the back and sleeves. The large button cost each man 6-cents and the small one 2 ½ -cents. The full set for three uniforms cost each cop $3.07.

When each policeman was fitted for his new buttons, he was given a diagram telling him how to use the button. The button was detachable and when the two parts of which it was formed were separated the policeman was instructed to push the fork of the front part through the cloth and then clasp it on the inside of the back of the button. The button could be detached only with a pin or some sharp instrument by means of a small automatic lock. If a policeman was to get into a fight with a prisoner there was little chance he could save his button, as they could be ripped off his uniform with ease. The instructional diagram revealed that the buttons were manufactured by the Automatic Button Company of Manhattan. [61]

Whether Murphy was pre-disposed to graft or was influenced by the well-heeled Devery remains a mystery. Regardless, Murphy may have recognized the opportunity to utilize his position for his own financial benefit, as allegations were unofficially made that he took a "cut" on all of the buttons purchased. If the allegations were true, unlike Devery whose graft and corrupt practices brought him tens, if not hundreds, of thousands of dollars, Murphy would have made his button money penny by penny.

Chapter 9: The Election of 1901

After the election of Mayor Van Wyck in 1897 the Citizens' Union wisely decided to keep in touch with the 150,000 independent voters who supported Seth Low. For this purpose, it created a permanent organization. In the campaigns of 1898 and 1899 it had cooperated with the local Bar Association, the City Club, and the Republican County Committee in the election of justices of the Supreme Court. Meanwhile Mayor Van Wyck displaced former Mayor Strong's heads of departments, and by appointing Jacob Hess, a Republican, to the bi-partisan police board, he carried out Tammany's mandate to install the notorious William Devery as chief of police, despite the fact that he had been dismissed from the department in 1894. The forced retirement of Chief of Police McCullagh and Devery's resurrection was a very unpopular move with most of the citizens of New York and would come back to bite Tammany. A greater surprise than the return of Big Bill Devery was the Tammany candidate to run against Seth Low.

After two years of press allegations and state investigations against Tammany Hall corruption, Republicans, independents, and anti-Tammany Democrats put aside their differences to nominate reformer Seth Low for mayor in 1901. The search for a clean mayoral candidate to counter the forces arrayed against Tammany Hall led Boss Richard Croker to offer the Tammany nomination to Edward M. Shepard, a well-respected lawyer and Democratic reformer who had previously denounced Tammany and backed Low's unsuccessful bid for the mayoralty in 1897.

Edward Morse Shepard was born in New York City in 1850. His father died when Edward was six years old, and August Belmont became legal guardian of the Shepard children. Raised in Brooklyn, Edward Shepard attended the common schools and City College, from which he graduated with the highest distinction in 1869. Afterward, he read law at a private firm and passed the state bar in 1871.

In 1895, Shepard ran unsuccessfully for the Brooklyn mayoralty against the Democratic machine of Hugh McLaughlin. The next year, Harper's Weekly deemed him a worthy leader of the reform Democrats, whose high character, as well as his eminent ability, commands the absolute confidence of his followers—in fact, of the community at large.

When the opportunity came to run for mayor of New York City in 1901, Shepard's commitment to reforming the Democratic Party from within compelled him to accept the Tammany nomination. Given the egregious corruption revealed through press and public investigations, many who previously held Shepard in high regard considered his candidacy to be naive or duplicitous. Harper's Weekly editorialized that his decision to run on a Tammany slate was personally "despicable" and "pathetic from the standpoint of public morals."

"What is he going to do?" asked the New York Times. "Manifestly he favors Tammany. He lends his distinguished name to that band of desperadoes to save them from impending destruction, to keep them alive and out of jail for two years." The Sun said, "He surrenders his good name for the sake of a chance to get office. The more people thought of his sacrifice, the more it seemed to them the work of ambition. Shepard owes his nomination to the coalition between Tammany, rotten to the core, and the McLaughlin machine of Brooklyn, just as corrupt, but not quite as brazen and obtuse. It is not possible for him to give the city good government with the tools these organizations have placed at his disposal."

During the campaign, Shepard had to deal with his past statements where he had frequently declared that Tammany Hall was " the disintegrating and corrupting power " in the city. When asked by a reporter of the Herald if he intended, in the event of his election, to retain Devery, he replied : "That is a hypothetical question. I have nothing to say on the subject." To this the Press retorted, "He is the thinnest veil ever used to mask the face of a political burglar entering a municipal household." Never did a local election in New York City excite more active interest.

Shepard also had to deal with the growing number of prominent citizens supporting Seth Low. During his campaign, he had the support of humorist Mark Twain. He and Twain made a joint appearance that drew a crowd of more than 2,000. In his own indomitable style, Twain made the following speech about the police bill that was to create a single headed police commissioner and abolish Devery's chief of police position:

"My scheme was to have only authors in the bill. For myself, I wanted to be the chief of force - not because I was particularly qualified, but because I was tired and wanted to rest. And I wanted Mr. Howells for First Deputy, not because he has any police ability, but because he's tired too. And I wanted Mr. Depew to be my Second Deputy, not because he's tired, but because he can do most anything well, and I could draw the salary. Then, he and I are members of the famous class of '53 at Yale, though he was there before I was.

"Then, again, Senator Depew is a Missouri man, the same as I am, and in a Missourian there is no guile. There is, too, a further bond of union in that when I was young, I was a member of a firm of twins, and one of them disappeared. There seems to me to be a resemblance in Senator Depew to me in grace of motion and fluency of speech. Which seems to me to designate him as that long-lost twin.

"Then in my Police bill I wanted Stedman, and Aldrich and Matthews for the Broadway squad, and others still for the 'Red Light' district, and others to look after the pretty manicurists, and to modify the activities of the cadets. Now, Depew could do that.

"Now that bill was my bright dream and my ambition. But it faded as so many other bright dreams have faded. Gov. Odell couldn't favor it. He said he couldn't leave the city unprotected. Now, I have nothing to do

*tomorrow and if the Governor will just hold a conference with me, we'll
settle the police question.*

*"If my bill passed I'd just fill up the 'Red Light' district with poets -
the best poets we've got - armed not with barbaric clubs, but with their
own poems, and I would make them corral those poor unkempt people of
that locality and I would have my poetic policemen read their poems to
them until that region was so elevated and uplifted and reformed that the
inhabitants over there themselves wouldn't know it."*

In November 1901, Shepard lost to Low, 53%-47%. The result was
a stunning blow. Tammany had the offices, the police, the prestige of
four years of absolute control, and an unlimited bank account, but one
day's fall of the ballots buried them. In Greater New York the fusionists
elected the mayor, comptroller, president of the board of aldermen,
and three of the five borough presidents, besides all county officers
and three out of four judges of the Supreme Court in the first judicial
district. It was an uprising of the common people.

Shepard attributed his defeat chiefly to Devery and Justice Jerome.
"With singular fatuity, under the goading of the press," he wrote,
"Devery indulged, until the eve of election, in crude utterances which
strengthened the impression of his abuses and oppressions. His very
energy seemed to possess a baneful fury exquisitely disturbing to every
person intelligently concerned for Democratic success. Jerome's
speeches, sounding the single note of a corrupt alliance between crime
and the police force, became the dominant feature near the end of the
struggle." [62]

Chapter 10: Exit

With the election of Seth Low, Murphy knew his tenure as police commissioner was finished. One of the most effective arguments for the election of Low's fusion ticket was his declaration that he would put an end to "Deveryism" by driving Big Bill Devery out of the police department. In fact, Devery had become an important issue in the campaign. Since Murphy was responsible for keeping Devery in the department by appointing him as his first deputy commissioner, he accepted that he would be gone as soon as Low took office. The only action Murphy took was to forestall his removal by Mayor Low by sending his letter of resignation to Mayor Van Wyck "to take effect upon the appointment of my successor." Murphy did not want to be in the position to be removed from office as Devery would be.

When asked by reporters about the prospects of his resignation, Devery snapped, "Me, resign? Me leave the police department? Never! I've said all along that I was here to stay, and I haven't changed my mind."

Mayor elect Low had already stated his intention to appoint Colonel John N. Partridge as police commissioner. John Nelson Partridge was the police commissioner for Brooklyn and fire commissioner for Brooklyn in the 1880s before the merger into New York City. He was the New York superintendent of public works before being tapped by Seth low to be police commissioner of New York City.

Devery's exit strategy was explained by his attorney, Abram I. Elkus. "Devery will make a formal protest to Commissioner Partridge and then vacate. The contention is that the law that legislated Devery out of office as chief of police is unconstitutional. I believe the courts will reinstate Devery. Whether Devery will hold his place after reinstatement, or will retire on a pension, depends on himself." [63]

The new year of 1902 got off to a delayed start at the mayor's office in City Hall. Mayor Low was delayed and did not get a chance to swear in Colonel Partridge as the new police commissioner until after 1 P.M. At that time an informal resignation was received from second deputy commissioner York, but Partridge did not want to proceed to police headquarters until a formal resignation was received from York. The formal resignation was important to Partridge because it would relieve him from having to remove York from office before appointing his own second deputy commissioner.

Meanwhile, at police headquarters Commissioner Murphy, Devery and a few of their friends sat anxiously for over two hours waiting for the arrival of the new commissioner, talking in low tones in an atmosphere similar to a funeral. Present with Devery was his lawyer, Abram I. Elkus. From time-to-time Devery would turn to his attorney and ask how he should act and what he should say when Colonel Partridge arrived. Devery's primary purpose at the impending meeting was to present Partridge with a formal letter of protest that had been prepared by his lawyer. The protest declared that Devery was the rightful chief of police, and that the law which had legislated him out of office was unconstitutional.

As the hours passed Murphy became impatient and blurted out that he didn't intend to wait much longer. Finally, at 2:30 P.M. the new police commissioner stepped into his new office.

"We're going to send you a bill for the day," Murphy sarcastically commented. He sat at his desk for the final time, presiding over a dramatic scene. In the big chair to his left sat Devery, uncharacteristically nervous and trembling. Attorney Elkus stood behind Devery, keeping a hand on the outgoing deputy commissioner's broad shoulder. Murphy's caregiver, Mr. Bacon, sat on the retiring commissioner's right.

Colonel Partridge was immediately apologetic about arriving late. "Mr. York sent me his resignation, but it was informal. That kept us," Partridge explained. "I wanted to have that arranged so that I wouldn't have to remove him."

Murphy rose and edged away from the desk, giving Colonel Partridge a chance to sit down, saying at the same time in a voice that quivered a little, "I want to offer you the hospitality of this room and to introduce you to Deputy Commissioner Devery."

"How are you, Mr. Devery?" Partridge greeted.

Devery half rose out of his chair and extended his huge hand. "I'm pleased to meet you," said Devery, his body shaking and his jaw working tremulously. He had a paper in his left hand that he passed to Colonel Partridge. "I just want to hand you my protest," he said before taking a different seat in the corner of the office. Partridge held onto the protest as he removed his overcoat. He then settled behind his new desk as he dropped the protest on the desktop.

Colonel Kipp, the chief clerk of the police department accepted the new commissioner's certificate of appointment and placed it on file. Commissioner Partridge then issued an order appointing Colonel N.B. Thurston and Major F.H.E. Ebstein as the first and second deputy commissioners. Partridge then picked up Devery's protest and began reading it.

Attorney Elkus tapped Devery's shoulder, prompting him to rise and say, "As a member of the uniformed force, I present myself for duty."

Partridge put down the letter of protest. "You say you are the chief of police and I say you are not. That will be for the courts to settle."

Attorney Elkus joined the conversation. "You understand, Colonel Partridge, that we are merely proceeding in a legal way to protect Devery's rights."

"I understand," Partridge nodded. He then shook hands with Devery before the former deputy commissioner walked out of the office as a private citizen. As he left the building, Devery was besieged by reporters for a statement, but the only comment he made was, "It's a damned cold day."

While Murphy was making his exit, he responded to the reporters' inquiries. "The only man I had any conflict with during my time as commissioner was Deputy Commissioner Devery. Mr. Devery and I had a great many differences of opinion in the department which we had to argue out. My personal relations with the deputy commissioner are very amicable, although the deputy commissioner has been pugnacious. I believe a great deal of the difference was caused by the deputy commissioner's belief that he is still chief of police. Personally, we are the best of friends."

A reporter asked what business Murphy was going into. "I'm going to take a good rest when I get out of here," he said. "I don't know what I will do after that."

"Have you made any business arrangements?" a reporter asked.

"None," he said as he exited police headquarters. [64]

Chapter 11: Aftermath

Throughout his time as police commissioner, Murphy maintained his position as leader of the First District. While Shepard unsuccessfully tried to win the mayoral election, Murphy attempted to hang onto his leadership of the First District. The fight that Colonel Murphy made at the primary election to hold his office was a struggle which impaired his strength to a great degree and probably hastened his death. He left not a stone unturned, but despite the activities of his lieutenants and his veteran generalship, his rival, Daniel E. Finn, better known in the area as "Battery Dan," defeated him. [65]

After years of physical weakness, when he battled for his life with a persistency which caused physicians to wonder, taking all his nutriment through a silver tube, and yet never till the very last losing his hold on Tammany politics.

His figure had been prominent in the first assembly district, and his career had been interwoven with its political battles, that even small boys could tell stories all day about "the old man" as he was sometimes called. This expression was even repeated by his old acquaintances nearly half a century later, when Mike Murphy the printer had become police commissioner and Justice Jerome and the committee of fifteen were raiding gambling houses and other disreputable places right under his nose.

In the latter days of his life, Murphy was famous for strong, black cigars, which he smoked. Unable to taste anything, he was deprived of the pleasure of eating and drinking. For the purpose, therefore, of obtaining some substitute he took to smoking, and the stronger the cigar the greater was the satisfaction which he seemed to derive from it.

At the democratic club one night, Croker invited Murphy and Larry Delmour "upstairs" for a conference.

Larry "Whispering Larry" Delmour was the long-time leader of the twenty-fourth district, and many considered him to be Croker's closest friend. At the conference, Croker offered his two associates a couple of fine cigars, handsomely wrapped in tinfoil.

"These are the best Havana cigars on the market," said Croker. "They cost fifty cents straight and were given to me by a cigar man that wants to get a friend into the Bridge Department."

Mr. Delmour took his cigar, brushed a few tears from his eyes as an acknowledgement of his thanks, and after whispering something, began to smoke. Murphy smoked his cigar for a time without a word, when Delmour whispered, "See there, the Colonel is smoking two cigars."

Investigation showed the charge was true, and Murphy was compelled to bring to view another cigar, which was so black and the fumes of which were so excessively strong that it started the whispering Larry to weeping afresh.

"Are you trying to spoil the cigar I gave you?" inquired Croker with a incredulous expression.

"No," was the answer, "but I thought it needed a tonic."

Murphy continually dealt with his diminished physical condition since 1889, but on January 26th, 1903, he was feeling particularly ill and fatigued as he sat in Tammany Hall. He returned home and for the next month complained of aggravation of his gastric disturbance. During the afternoon of March 4th, while sitting up in bed, being attended to by his caregiver, Mr. Bacon, he suddenly became unconscious and died several hours later. [66]

There was one more surprise in the story of Police Commissioner Michael C. Murphy. Most of his friends and associates believed Murphy to be a bachelor, but at his funeral, not one, but two women appeared who claimed to be his wife. Kate Clements, who was said to be Murphy's second wife, brought with her their original marriage certificate, documenting the marriage on February 19, 1870, in Albany. Mrs. Clements, whose second husband, Colonel Addison Clements died fourteen years earlier, said she met Colonel Murphy at a dinner in

Central Park in 1868, and for two years they corresponded with each other. While Murphy was attending the Legislature in February 1870, Mrs. Clements visited Albany, and as the marriage notice showed, they were married on February 19th. Mrs. Clements said that she and Murphy returned to New York City and lived very happily for five or six years at 67 Varick Street. [67]

Also at the funeral was a heavily veiled woman who identified herself as Mary Drennan, Murphy's first wife. After Murphy returned from Albany with his second wife on his arm in 1870, Mary moved out and remained in New York, but never spoke to Murphy again.

Both widows unsuccessfully sued for Murphy's estate, which in his will, he had left entirely to his caregiver of many years, Frank L. Bacon. [68]

There was some question as to the value of the estate Mr. Bacon inherited. By some accounts, Murphy's estate was valued at only $2,000, but other accounts mentioned real estate in Manhattan, the Bronx, and Far Rockaway valued in excess of $150,000.[69]

Michael Cotter Murphy was buried at Kensico Cemetery in Valhalla, New York. [70]

...

With Seth Low's victory came the ousting of the city police commissioner, Michael C. Murphy, and his brazenly corrupt deputy, William "Big Bill" Devery.

Low introduced a merit-based civil service system, hired municipal employees and eliminated graft within the police department. He also improved the education system within the city and lowered taxes. Nevertheless, he only served for two years and was defeated by Democrat George B. McClellan, Jr. in 1903.

But what became of Big Bill Devery after he was dumped from the police department. When he was given his walking papers from police headquarters by Mayor Low, Devery was a very rich man with a mansion and a real estate business in Far Rockaway. Big Bill was not done with politics, however. He had more he wanted to do.

Devery ran for District Leader in the Ninth Assembly District. Richard Croker had been removed from power in Tammany Hall and Tammany's new leadership did not provide the support Big Bill had grown accustomed to. Devery had to finance his own campaign, which meant he had to use his own money to buy votes. Devery threw a huge party attended by over 18,000 people, complete with food, bars, music, and fireworks – all for free. Instead of a speech, Big Bill told the crowd that he would love it if the crowd would vote for him and urge all their friends and relatives to also vote for him. Afterall, Devery knew no one came to here him speak, so he made his one pitch for votes and let the crowd have fun. Devery threw a second party where he went through 20,000 glasses of beer, 1,700 pounds of roast beef, and 15,000 rolls. On election day, Big Bill won in a landslide against the Tammany candidate. Somehow, Devery had garnered more votes than there were people in the district. In his triumph, Devery marched through the streets with a big brass band as throngs of people lined the streets to cheer.

By this point, Devery had been cast aside by new Tammany boss Charles F. Murphy. Although Devery had won the election, he was not able to take his seat, for he was ousted by the Tammany Election Committee. They accused him of encouraging voter fraud. Spurned, Devery broke from the Democratic Party and prepared to run for mayor in 1903 as an independent candidate.

Devery created his own political party – the Independent People's Party. The symbol of the party was, what else, the pump. His headquarters was Devery's bar, which had been nicknamed "the Bug House." Running for mayor on the slogan, "Have a drink on me," Devery came in sixth out of seven entries, getting just 2,960 votes. And with that, Devery's political career had run its course. But Big

Bill was not going to slowly fade away from the public eye. With his accumulated fortune, Big Bill Devery still had big plans.

While Seth Low had set his sights on eliminating the corruption that had been so prevalent, Devery was closing a deal that would make him co-owner of the New York Highlanders baseball team, a team that would eventually change its name to the Yankees.

Context about this transaction must begin in 1902, when American League President Ban Johnson sought to move a struggling Baltimore franchise to New York. To help bypass former New York Giants owner Andrew Freedman, who wanted to protect new owner John T. Bush's interests by staving off other ball clubs, Johnson entertained offers from potential investors for a New York team, eventually landing on gambler and pool hall/casino owner Frank J. Farrell. And for some unknown — perhaps political — reason, Farrell chose Devery as his business partner.

Before the 1903 season, Johnson agreed to sell the Baltimore club to Farrell and Devery for $18,000 — not including the costs of moving the team, purchasing land and building a ballpark.

Because of Devery's nefarious past and Farrell's connection to New York's vice underworld, Johnson wanted to cloak the pair's ownership of the team — and did so by arranging for Manhattan coal broker Joseph Gordon to become the team's president. Also a realtor, Gordon was able to secure a lease at a Washington Heights property owned by the New York Institute for the Blind. The owners secured a 10-year lease and the team that played on the grounds would soon be known as the New York Highlanders. On this property, Farrell, Devery and Gordon built Hilltop Park. Though Devery and Farrell were not listed on the club's incorporation papers, journalists soon caught on to the trickery. The two sat in the owners' box on Opening Day 1903.

The Highlanders finished their inaugural season over .500 and almost earned a pennant the next season. But after that, it was all downhill. Farrell disposed of Gordon and took on the role of team president himself. Meanwhile, Devery stuck to his real-estate affairs in Manhattan and Far Rockaway.

By the end of the decade, Farrell was in a financial bind thanks to the Manhattan DA's casino crackdown. The state legislature also closed racetracks with which Farrell frequently did business. At the same time, Farrell was forced to foot the bill for expensive renovations at Hilltop Park. The ballpark's lease was up in 1912, and the Institute for the Blind announced there would be no renewal. So, Farrell financed a new park in the Bronx.

The Highlanders were renamed the Yankees and played their 1913 season at the Polo Grounds. Devery was still a nonfactor, going on to purchase a minor league club called the Jersey City Skeeters. He would later abandon that team.

During the 1914 season, Devery was involved in a clubhouse brawl with the Yankees' manager Frank Chance. Chance had already won a championship with the Chicago Cubs when he signed a three-year contract with the Yankees in 1913. The Yankees sat in last place on the next-to-last day of the 1913 season but won their final game to finish in seventh place. After struggling during the 1914 season, Chance resigned with three weeks left in the season and the Yankees mired in seventh place.

Contributing to Chance's departure from the team was an encounter with Devery at the Polo Grounds after a game. Chance had already communicated his intention to resign, partially due to the meddling of Devery, who considered himself an expert baseball strategist. Chance believed Devery was undermining him with his players with his "grandstand managing."

Chance was addressing reporters in the clubhouse regarding his decision to resign when Devery entered and called Chance a quitter. Harsh words were exchanged until Chance threw a wild punch at Devery that failed to connect. The two men were the pulled apart before any further blows could be attempted.

This encounter, some believe, catalyzed the owners' departures from the club. Farrell had the press to deal with, while Devery attempted to solve a financial obligation to his Skeeters team.

By the end of the 1914 season, Devery was more or less an outcast. Farrell, though, was devoted to the team. With no other lucrative offers, the pair sold the team to brewery owner Jacob Ruppert and construction engineer Til Huston for around $460,000.

Devery lived out the last few years of his life in relative obscurity. He became obese, battling illness in 1918-19 which resulted in heart disease. On June 20, 1919, he suffered a stroke in his Far Rockaway home and died at the age of 65. Around ten years later, it was revealed that many of his assets were mortgaged, and he died slightly "in the red." [71]

Chapter 12: Legacy

What exactly is the legacy of the New York City Police Department's first commissioner? The answer is as complex as Michael Murphy's life.

Colonel Murphy was appointed as police commissioner for a purpose, and in a sense, he accomplished that purpose well. Clearly, his physical limitations made it difficult, if not impossible to perform the job efficiently, but if he had been a vigorous and capable man, he would have been distinctly ineligible for the position. Big Bill Devery had all the vigor and capacity needed to preserve the traditions of the force and take care of those "higher ups." Murphy was not one of those occupying this higher plane. His salary of $7,500 per year was "all there was in it" for him, and about seven thousand five hundred times as much as he could probably earn outside of politics. Croker knew what he was about when he arranged to have Murphy appointed.

If the management of the police force of New York had been a task comparable to the organization of a picnic for aged and indigent females, Colonel Murphy would have done very well, and it was probably in the hope that he would regard it in this light that he was chosen. His amiable assurances of a purpose to make the force a model for the world were accepted with complacence by the public and with great amusement by the initiated. His official career as police commissioner was a series of contradictory statements and painful surprises, no doubt, but it was intended to be, provided events should render it necessary to have a figurehead to take the pounding of public criticism.

As far as accomplishments were concerned, one could point to Murphy's institution of the three-platoon system for policemen, but even that action was steeped in shady politics.

Until 1901 the police force worked under a two-platoon system. Under this system the command of each precinct was divided into two platoons of two sections each. This system required policemen to work long hours on patrol and in reserve. For years the cops had petitioned for a three-platoon system where cops would work 8-hour shifts.

Transitioning to three platoons would require more policemen and would therefore, be a very expensive proposition. The policemen initially tried to obtain the three-platoon system through legislation in Albany, but this effort failed. Mayor Van Wyck and Tammany Hall weren't very interested in absorbing the expense of the three-platoon system, even if it could secure the votes of the police. But then something amazing happened. During the time the policemen had been petitioning Albany, they had set up a "Persuasion Fund." Every policeman had contributed $15 to the fund to help persuade the legislature to pass the bill. Tammany Hall suddenly realized that this money had never been used, and $90,000 was just sitting there for them.

Commissioner Murphy became a vocal supporter of the three-platoon system and put it into operation in August 1901, despite the added cost.

When he took office, Police Commissioner Partridge quickly abolished the three-platoon system. The reasons Partridge cited about the expense of the plan were exactly in line with what the Tammany officials said when it looked as if the patrolmen might get the favor they desired from the state legislature. Colonel Murphy, himself, had denounced the three-platoon system, and declared that it would cost the city millions of dollars. When, however, the bill was beaten in Albany and the Tammany officials found that the fund raised among the patrolmen, had not been returned to the contributors, and was still available for those who could secure the adoption of the three-platoon system, they became enthusiastic advocates of the plan. Colonel Murphy was persuaded that it was the up-to-date method of conducting the police force and announced that it could be put in perfect operation without increase in the number of patrolmen or any additional cost to the city. Murphy must have known what the system would really cost, but he would be out of office in a few months, and it would be a problem for another commissioner. Partridge found that it would require 1,605 additional patrolmen at an added expense of $2,039,463, and a further expense of about $500,000 for new sergeants and roundsmen, to give the city the same protection that it had under the old system. [72]

Commissioner Murphy probably knew about the practical workings of the police system only what he read in the newspapers, and of this he believed only so much as he had to. He was in many respects the most pathetic figure in the city government at the time. The sarcasm of the Merchant's Association was wasted on him.

Michael C. Murphy was not an evil or inherently corrupt man. He was a product of the times when corrupt activities in New York City politics was "business as usual." To blame Murphy too severely for the corruption in the police department during his tenure as commissioner would be a substantial injustice. He could no more initiate and carry out the necessary measures of reform demanded by the condition of the police force than a fly on a coach wheel could change the direction of its revolution. But there is one achievement that can never be taken away from Michael Cotter Murphy. He was New York City's first police commissioner. [73]

Chapter 13: The Cartoon Story

Political cartoons are an integral component in the framework of political journalism. They offer a brightly colored alternative to formal news reporting, providing light relief from the ever-increasingly gloomy political discourse. With the ability to distil news and opinion into a caricature, cartoons present accessible and instant commentary and analysis of current affairs.

Cartoons are a unique form of journalism which contrast with conventional forms of communication. The images can cast a powerful interpretation on the day's news. They explain and explore stories in manners that articles cannot. More effective than writing or video, they capture the imitable human nature of their subjects in order to humanize the topic they depict.

The satirical character of this form of journalism adds to its appeal. By combining humor with the latest political news, cartoonists can reinforce their messaging, focusing on the frequently ridiculous nature of stories.

As can be seen in the newspapers during the 19th and early 20th centuries, cartoons did not only act as news sources, but they created a historical record of the political climate. This was particularly true with the issue of police corruption in New York City in 1901 and the depiction of Tammany Hall, Richard Croker, Police Commissioner Murphy, and Deputy Commissioner Devery, who was something of a cartoon-like character in real life.

Most people today don't fully understand the power of these early political cartoons. We take literacy for granted, but in 1870, 20% of the population of the United States could not read or write and by 1900 over 10% of the population was illiterate. For some people, cartoons in newspapers were the only mode of communication. William "Boss" Tweed, the legendary corrupt politician who ruled New York's

Tammany Hall during the late 19th Century before Richard Croker, was literally brought down by cartoons. The series of drawings exposing the Tweed Ring was produced by political cartoonist Thomas Nast in *Harper's Weekly*. So effective were his images in rousing public opinion, Mr. Tweed was reported to have said "Let's stop those damned pictures. I don't care so much what the papers write about me — my constituents can't read, but damn it, they can see pictures."

The story I have just told of the tenure of New York City's first single-headed police commissioner. Michael Murphy, and his First Deputy Commissioner, Big Bill Devery, could just as easily have been told through cartoons in lieu of text. Let's see.

This cartoon appeared at the time in 1894 when Devery was convicted of extortion and bribery and was about to be dismissed from the police department.

As depicted in this cartoon, by 1901 Devery's collusion with illegal gambling houses was common knowledge.

COMMISSIONER OF POLICE M. C. MURPHY.
(Sketched from life at his home last evening)

This is one of the most flattering depictions of Murphy after his appointment as police commissioner. It contains his statement that very few believed that he alone was the chief of police.

This cartoon makes fun of Murphy's statement that he didn't believe illegal gambling houses existed in the city.

COL. MURPHY IN HIS OFFICE.

This was cartoonist T.E. Long's impression of his first meeting with Commissioner Murphy. Note the frail appearance of Murphy and how the commissioner is relegated to sitting outside First Deputy Commissioner Devery's office, with the rest of Devery's goons.

This carton depicts the mountain of evidence of illegal gambling being poured on Murphy's head after he stated he could find no illegal gambling in the city.

"SOLOMON" DEVERY IN ACTION.

One of Devery's roles as First Deputy Commissioner was to preside of department trials. This cartoon spoofs the "wise" judge.

This cartoon depicts Tammy Boss Croker using his tentacles to reach out to all areas of city government to line his pockets.

The feeble Murphy is nothing more than a trained monkey being led on a leash by Devery as he stands before the bar of justice. Note that the scales of justice are more heavily weighted toward Devery's neglect of duty.

This cartoon appeared after Devery was appointed First Deputy Commissioner. It depicts Commissioner Murphy, the Tammany Tiger, and Richard Croker observing Devery, who is seated on a throne, being handed a document from a kneeling Father Knickerbocker, the symbol of New York City at the time. The document is Father Knickerbocker's resignation to the fact that Devery was not going anywhere.

COL. MURPHY AND MOSS.

"Col. Murphy, would you give Mr. Moss a job on the police force?"
"I will, if he can pass the Civil Service Board."
This is a sketch of the Civil-Service Board the Colonel must have had in his mind when he spoke—a sort of third-degree-say-call-for-the ambulance!

With reform activist and attorney Frank Moss being such a thorn in the side of Murphy, Devery, and the police department, when Murphy said Moss could work for the department if he passed the civil service board, this was the artist's depiction of the type of board that would await Moss.

Artist's depiction of hatchet wielding activist Carrie Nation's visit to police headquarters.

This cartoon appeared when Devery was voted out of his position as the president of the Association of Police Chiefs.

Devery's fairy godmother, who happens to resemble a deck of cards, rains a fortune down on Devery.

When the scandal involving tips of raids being called to gambling houses via the police headquarters phone line broke, this cartoon depicts the emaciated Murphy cluelessly standing by while Devery phones in a tip to a gambling house.

This cartoon again shows the clueless commissioner vowing to investigate while Devery runs the pool room "tip" phone line.

This cartoon speaks for itself.

Before he was identified as the primary "tipster" to the gambling houses of impending raids, Patrolman Edward Glennon (good friend of Devery) was known as Joe Doe.

"TOUCHIN' ON AND APPERTAININ' TO"—
Deputy Chief Devery.

This cartoon was published after Glennon received a 6-month sentence for his role in the "tipping" scandal

"There have been a lot of these philanthropists who have been putting a lot of hurdles in the way of the Police Department, but we manage to jump them all."

As Parkhurst and Moss watch, this cartoon depicts Murphy and Devery attempting to avoid and hop past every scandal that appeared before them.

"'NEATH THE SHADE OF THE SHELTERING (ITCHING) PALM"

This cartoon shows the protective hand of the police department watching over the illegal activities.

The cartoonish Devery was also used in campaign literature for Seth Low.

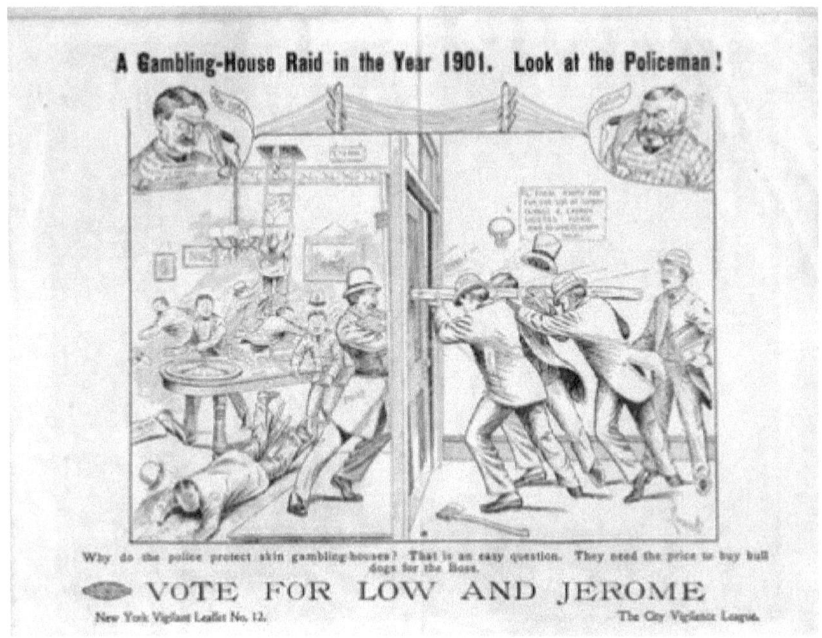

Another Seth Low campaign poster depicting the police protecting a gambling house from a raid.

A MARRIAGE OF CONVENIENCE

This cartoon comically portrays the "Marriage of Convenience" between Tammany and Edward Shepard, with the carefree and dapper candidate holding the paw of the veiled Tammany Tiger. In the background behind the couple, an irritable Croker carries a model of City Hall, and behind him a worried-looking Police Chief Devery bears a bouquet of flowers. The "Made In England" ribbon on Shepard's coat may allude to his aristocratic manner.

This illustration depicts the club of Big Bill Devery and those he either "clubbed" with his authority, or would like to club, including Patrolman O'Neill, Patrolman Monahan, Patrolman Marrinan, and ADA Osborne.

The cartoon version of the changing of the guard when Colonel Partridge took over as police commissioner and introduced Colonel Thurston as his first deputy commissioner.

The unrefined Devery comically responds to the military bearing of new Police Commissioner Partridge

This cartoon shows gambling going on unmolested while Mayor Van Wyck presents a medal to Devery proclaiming him the "Best Chief of Police New York ever had."

Justice has removed the mask of the police department revealing that Devery is nothing more than the Tammany Tiger.

Photo Gallery

A young healthy Murphy contrasted with the older unhealthy version.

Murphy during the Civil War.

MRS. KATE CLEMENTS.
(From a photograph taken at the time of her marriage.)

Murphy's second wife.

Big Bill Devery

Devery (B) and Frank Farrell (A) as baseball club owners.

Frank Chance – manager of the Yankees involved in a brawl with Devery.

Richard Croker

Frank Moss

Justice William Jerome

BERNARD J. YORK.

Colonel Partridge and his deputy commissioners

LIEUT.-COL. THURSTON.

MAJOR FRED H. E. EBSTEIN.

WARDMAN EDWARD G. GLENNON.

POLICEMAN ONEILL.

Mayor Robert Van Wyck

Police Headquarters – 300 Mulberry Street

Bibliography

1. Citron, New York Exposed
2. Felt, Jeremy P., Vice Reform as a Political Technique: The Committee of Fifteen in New York, 1900-1901, Vol. 54, No. 1 (JANUARY 1973), Cornell Press, pp. 24-51
3. Keire, Mara Laura, For Business and Pleasure, John Hopkins University Press, 2010, p13
4. Myers, Gustavus, History of Tammany Hall, 2012, p289
5. New York Tribune 3/8/1903, p14
6. The New York Times, 3/2/1860, p2
7. Brooklyn Daily Eagle, 8/7/1879, p2
8. New York Tribune, 6/8/1866, p4
9. The Sun, 3/11/1903, p4
10. New York Tribune, 1/9/1897, p4
11. New York Tribune, 1/1/1901, p1
12. New York Tribune, 1/12/1901, p3
13. New York Tribune, 1/2/1901, p1
14. New York Tribune, 1/12/1901, p1
15. New York Tribune, 1/5/1901, p1
16. New York Tribune, 1/10/1901, p1
17. Sheerin, James (1933). "Henry Codman Potter, an American Metropolitan". Fleming H. Revell Company.
18. New York Tribune, 1/13/1901, p5
19. New York Tribune, 1/28/1901, p12
20. New York Tribune, 1/30/1901, p1
21. New York Tribune, 2/7/1901, p4
22. New York Tribune, 2/19,1901, p5
23. New York Tribune, 2/12/1901, p3
24. New York Tribune, 2/23/1901, p2
25. New York Tribune, 2/23/1901, p2
26. The New York Times, 10/26/1909, p9
27. New York Tribune, 2/23/1901, p2

28. New York Tribune, 2/24,1901, p1
29. New York Tribune, 2/24/1901, p2
30. New York Tribune, 2/24/1901, p2
31. The NYPD's First Fifty Years: Politicians, Police, p13
32. New York Tribune, 2/26/1901, p8
33. The World, 3/1/1901, p2
34. New York Tribune, 2/23/1901, p2
35. New York Tribune, 3/4/1901, p5
36. New York Tribune, 3/4/1901, p1
37. New York Tribune, 3/4/1901, p2
38. New York Tribune, 3/10/1901, p4
39. New York Tribune, 3/13/1901, p4
40. Ten Months of Tammany, City Club of New York, Oct. 1901
41. Bowery Boys, Crazy Hatchet Lady, October 3, 2011
42. Brooklyn Daily Eagle, 8/30/1901, p1
43. The World, 9/12/1901, p12
44. The Sun, 9/13/1901, p2
45. Munsey's Magazine, Volume 61, 1917, p641
46. The New York Times, 5/4/1901, p16
47. Brooklyn Daily Times, 9/25/1901, p1
48. The Brooklyn Daily Eagle, 10/22/1901. P24
49. The Brooklyn Daily Eagle, 11/9/1901. P1
50. The New York Times, 9/17/01, p14
51. The Brooklyn Times, 12/26/1901, p4
52. The Brooklyn Citizen, 5/20/1903, p6
53. The New York Times, 5/22/1901 p16
54. The New York Times, 8/10/1901 p2
55. The New York Times, 8/11/01 p1
56. The New York Times, 8/10/1901 p2
57. The New York Times, 8/16/1901 p12
58. The New York Times, 5/21/1901 p4
59. The Brooklyn Daily Eagle, 6/12/1901 p4

60. The Standard Union, 7/3/1901, p12

61. The Brooklyn Daily Eagle,10/3/1901 p20

62. Stanwood, The Political History of the State of New York, Vol. IV, 1883-1905

63. New York Tribune, 12/29/1901, p5

64. The Sun, 1/2/1902, p2

65. New York Tribune, 3/8/1903, p14

66. The New York Times, 3/5/1903, p9

67. The Evening World, 3/10/1903, p3

68. New York Tribune, 3/20/1903, p5

69. The Providence News, 6/9/1903, p7

70. The Evening World March 10, 1903, p3

71. Gunderman, Dan, New York Daily News, 2017

72. New York Tribune, 2/10/1902, p6

73. The New York Times, 9/5/1901, p6